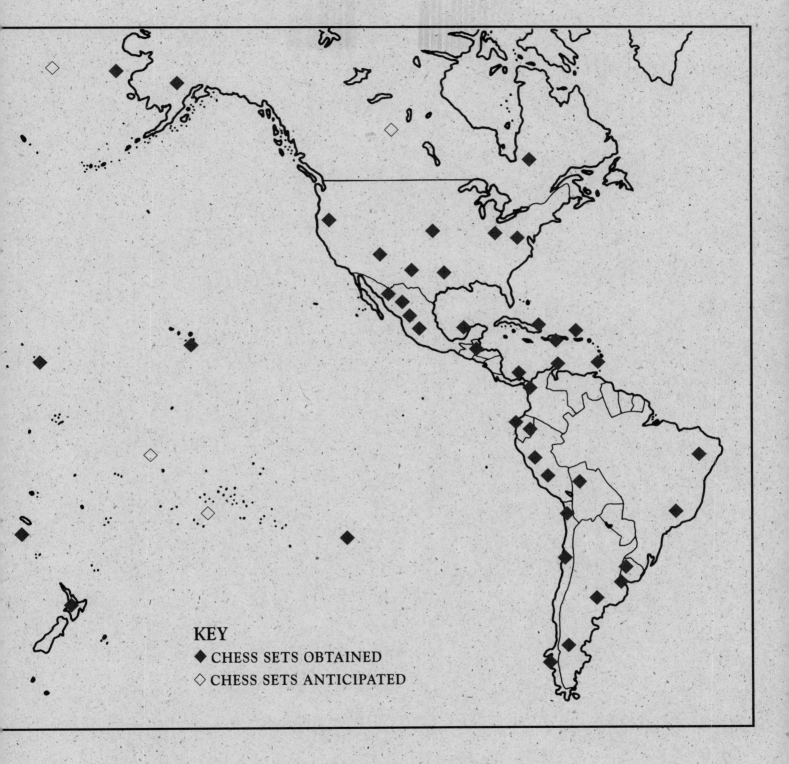

KEY
♦ CHESS SETS OBTAINED
◇ CHESS SETS ANTICIPATED

CULTURES, CHESS & ART

A COLLECTOR'S ODYSSEY ACROSS SEVEN CONTINENTS

VOLUME 1 SUB-SAHARAN AFRICA

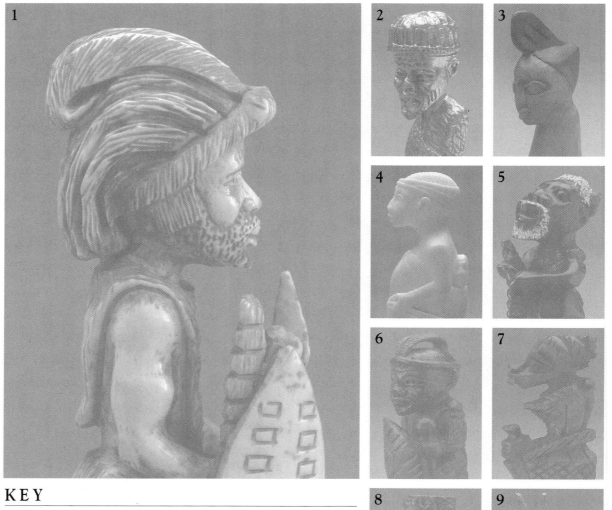

KEY

Cover Photographs

1. South Africa ◆ Zulu ◆ King ◆ Stained Ivory ◆ Page 101
2. Swaziland ◆ King ◆ Pewter ◆ Page 107
3. Sierra Leone ◆ Creole Pawn ◆ Wood ◆ Page 40
4. Congo ◆ Queen ◆ Ivory ◆ Page 52
5. Swaziland ◆ King ◆ Stone ◆ Page 107
6. Malawi ◆ Knight ◆ Serpentine ◆ Page 28
7. Malawi ◆ Queen ◆ Wood ◆ Page 29
8. Zambia ◆ Chokwe ◆ Queen ◆ Wood ◆ Page 54
9. Mali ◆ Knight ◆ Gold ◆ Page 42

PHOTOGRAPHY BY HAL SMITH ◆ DESIGN BY ROB ROEHRICK

CULTURES, CHESS & ART

A COLLECTOR'S ODYSSEY ACROSS SEVEN CONTINENTS

BY NED MUNGER

EDITED BY LISA A. SMITH

MUNDIAL PRESS, SAN ANSELMO, CALIFORNIA

VOLUME 1 SUB-SAHARAN AFRICA

NED MUNGER

is a California Institute of Technology professor emeritus who has written
numerous books and articles on the history, geography, and politics of Africa.
He is former president of the L. S. B. Leakey Foundation, a leader of State
Department missions to Africa, and current president of the Cape of Good
Hope Foundation.

Mundial Press
Carlson Court
P.O. Box 2543
San Anselmo, CA 94979

Printed in the United States of America

Publisher's Cataloging in Publication
(*Prepared by Quality Books Inc.*)

Munger, Edwin S., 1921–
    Cultures, chess & art: a collector's odyssey across seven continents.
Volume 1, Sub-Saharan Africa / by Ned Munger; edited by Lisa A. Smith.
    p. cm.
    Includes bibliographical references and index.
    LCCN: 95-81611.
    ISBN 0-9644046-6-4

    1. Chess sets--Africa, Sub-Saharan. 2. Art, African. 3. Munger, Edwin
S., 1921– 4. Africa, Sub-Saharan--Description and travel. 5. Africa, Sub-
Saharan--History.   I. Title. II. Title: Cultures, chess & art. III. Title: A
collector's odyssey across seven continents. IV. Title: Sub-Saharan Africa.

NK4696.M86 1996   731.8'9'7941
                                         QBI95-20771

♾ The paper used in this publication meets the minimum requirements of the
American National Standard for Information Sciences—Permanence of Paper for
Printed Library Materials, ANSI Z39.48-1992.

ACKNOWLEDGMENTS

Without the keen questioning, substantive and meticulous editing, and organizing by Lisa A. Smith of San Anselmo, California, this book would not be in print. Photographer Hal Smith of Los Angeles approached this project with his characteristic good humor, patience, and sharp eye for simplicity of light and design that lets the pieces speak for themselves. Designer Rob Roehrick of San Rafael, California drew upon his background and experience in fine arts and art history, with a special appreciation for African art, culture, and the game of chess, in designing this book.

Antique and chess set experts all over the world, and particularly the members of Chess Collectors International, have played an enormous role in providing information. Among those to whom I am most indebted for their special help are: in Germany, Wolfgang Angerstein, Franz Josef Lang, Thomas Thomsen, and Hans Joachim Tinti; in Switzerland, Ernst Boehlen; in England, Garrick Coleman, Penelope Higham, Victor Keats, Michael Mark, and Novello (Vel) and Gareth Williams; in the United States, Andreas Aebi, Betty Arends, Robert Bloch, George Dean, Erwin Ezzes, David Hafler, David Hapgood, George Hedges, Valentina Lindholm, Rosy Meiron, Kay Morry, Tania Norris, Carole Patton, Dorothy Raymond, Floyd and Berneice Sarisohn, Juliann Wolfram, and Juris Zurins.

Valuable knowledge about individual sets was contributed by many, including Gabeba Abrahams, Flick Asvat, Teresa Barclay, Donald Brody, Ian Lavaretto, Qondile Nxumalo, Madelaine Van Biljon, and Elsa Van Laere.

My research was greatly aided by the dedicated library staff at Caltech, including Janet Jenks, Judy Nollar, Kathleen Potter, and Mary Schaffler; the staff at Interlibrary Loan; and Charlene Baldwin, UC Riverside science librarian.

Victoria Mason provided invaluable secretarial and word processing help, as well as occasional editing, along with Eloisa Imel. Dorothy Raymond also performed occasional editing and generously contributed to finding sets. Bob Turring assisted with map making. ▣

CONTENTS

PREFACE

The purpose of these volumes is to present chess sets as works of art, to explain them as expressions of diverse cultures, and to foster an appreciation of the heuristic value inherent in collecting them.

My own appreciation of the educational value of chess set collecting has been deepened by association with various colleagues at the California Institute of Technology (Caltech), where I had the good fortune to teach African Studies from 1951 to 1990. You will meet some of those colleagues in these pages. I am also learning much through my association with members of Chess Collectors International, whose board I serve on as a "new boy."[1] You are encouraged to enlighten me further by contacting me about any misinformation you find in these books.

Ethnicity is the focus of my collection. You may ask, "What is ethnicity?" To me it is simply the characteristics that pertain to a people. Whether the people are English or German or Malay or Chinese or Easter Islanders, their culture and costumes and customs are "ethnic." The word *ethnic* does not attribute status; it does not imply a value judgment. Indeed, diversity and catholicity are part of the appeal of chess set art.

At one presentation of my sets a famous German collector of Meissen sets took umbrage at what he presumably saw as my classification of exquisite porcelain sets from the eighteenth century under the same rubric as crude contemporary African sets. His reaction may have been the result of a semantic problem: thinking of *Kultur* as opposed to folk art. Ethnic (cultural) difference is revealed, for example, in the dress of the eighteenth century court of Saxony as contrasted with the Moorish style of the opposing side in a famous Meissen set.

Without being anti-semantic, I accept the point that quality of art varies by individual and world standards. However, I do not judge the artistic value of the sets described in these volumes; rather I try to extract value from the judgments of the chess set makers themselves, even when they take a priapic turn, as in Bali.

The 1989 unabridged edition of the *Oxford English Dictionary* defines ethnic "as pertaining to nations not Christian or Jewish." However, it defines ethnography as "the scientific description of nations or races of men, with their customs, habits, and points of difference." It is in that second sense that I apply both words to my chess sets.

I am not ready to abandon the word *ethnic* because some treat it with derision or avoid it to be politically correct. When former Chancellor Franklin Murphy established the magnificent ethnic museum at the University of California, Los Angeles in 1963, it was called the Museum and Laboratories for Ethnic Art and Technology. Now, with substantially the same outstanding exhibits housed in a handsome new building, it is called the Museum of Cultural History. Deputy Director Ross disclaims a move to political correctness. To him, *ethnic* is pejorative: "To use the term 'ethnography' or 'ethnic art' is a mistake to my mind. That is how the dominant white cultures tend to marginalize other cultures." He points out that he comes from Norway, with four million inhabitants, and that Mexico has sixty-seven million. "Why," he asks, "is Norwegian art not 'ethnic,' and Mexican art is 'ethnic'?"

The answer, I believe, is that both are ethnic; and there is every reason for both populations to be proud of their artisans and craftspeople.

So, no, I will not change the name of my collection. It would be stilted to call it a "collection of cultural chess sets."

When I was six or seven my father taught me to play chess on a Staunton Jacques set that had been handed down by my grandfather. I acquired my first set during World War II while stationed at the Presidio in Monterey, California.[2]

My first wife, Elizabeth Nelson, worked in the Presidio library. Adalbert Schmidt, a German prisoner of war, also worked there. Elizabeth had been very kind to him, and when we left the Presidio he gave her a chess set that he had carved with a penknife—a pine set with a medieval German theme.[3]

Traveling the world and collecting chess sets are harmonious pursuits. The impetus to collect came, for me, in the 1950s and 1960s when I traveled a great deal on a Crane Rogers Foundation Fellowship and as an academic correspondent for the American Universities Field Staff. An increased understanding of Africa and its role in the world was the professional purpose of my visits to various capitals of the world. But there was always some free time. So I looked for local chess sets.

The search took me into areas of cities and countryside where tourists did not often venture—unfamiliar parts of Arusha, Auckland, Dublin, Istanbul, Lagos, Lima, Mandalay, Manila, Moscow, Oslo, Seoul, Shanghai, Tananarive, Tokyo, the Trobriand Islands—to name a few.

Serendipity sometimes triumphed and I found a set along the way. But an unsuccessful search was never a defeat. "To travel hopefully is a better thing than to arrive…The great affair is to move," wrote Robert Louis Stevenson. And move I did. Over more than forty years I traveled to Africa eighty-nine times and made innumerable trips to the other continents, visiting more than three hundred countries and major islands.

These volumes are, in part, a chronicle of those travels, the many rewarding friendships made, and the provocative conversations engaged in en route. Frequently I would be invited to dine with a designer or carver of chess sets, or with the owner of an antique or crafts shop where I had inquired about sets. At times I would share a pint of ale and converse with someone I had stopped to ask for directions. There were memorable visits with heads of state; moments of apprehension involving political intrigue; chance meetings with the well-known; and times of satisfaction when I was able to help the unknown along the way.

I hope you enjoy traveling through these volumes. As the Zulus urge their friends: *hamba gahle*, travel well. ▪

The origin of chess remains an unsolved puzzle; the Dead Sea Scrolls of chess history have not yet been found. However, discoveries—almost as revolutionary to chess as the Scrolls are to biblical knowledge—continue to emerge in India, the Middle East, Russia, and Europe. And hundreds of recondite tomes are available to serious scholars.[1]

Games in general go back to Pharaonic times. It was thought that the game of chess as we know it began in northwest India around 600 A.D. and then spread to Persia and Arabia. The Indians called the game *Chaturanga*. This refers, in Sanskrit, to a division of four, as used in the Indian army for its sections: infantry, cavalry, chariots, and elephants. However, there is no trail of evidence, in terms of chess pieces, that leads to India as the origin of the game.

The most recent scholarship, particularly that of British historian Kenneth Wilde and Spanish physician and International Grand Master Richard Calvo, suggests that chess more likely originated in Persia. A book by Calvo is forthcoming. He posits three reasons to support his belief that Persia was the source of the game: (1) most of the early literature refers to Persian chess; (2) the earliest pieces discovered so far, such as in Nishapur, tend to be Persian; and (3) the strong mathematical components of early chess, such as the permutations of the moves of the Knight, are more logically based on the state of mathematics knowledge in the Middle East rather than in India. I am inclined to support this new theory about the origin of chess.

The expression *check mate* is from the Arab *alsha mat* (the king is dead). An Omani chess set more than one thousand years old, just discovered in 1993, seems to bear out the presence of the game in that part of the world.

Islamic sets, created under the Prophet's injunction against representing the human figure, entered Spain with the Moors in approximately the tenth century.

More new evidence of chess in antiquity may be revealed by my colleague in Moscow, Professor Izak Linder, who has been active in excavating for ninth century pieces in the old Russian city of Novogorod. Linder's latest study sheds valuable new information on the origins of chess in Russia and contains copious color illustrations of some of the more modern sets.[2]

The most spectacular ancient chess pieces in Europe are the Charlemagne pieces at the Bibliotheque Nationale in Paris. Charlemagne, of course, was emperor of the Holy Roman Empire from 800 to 814. The ivory set was produced much later—probably in the eleventh century—in southern Italy, possibly in Amalfi, which was then the center for importation of ivory tusks from Africa. Magnificent works of art, the Charlemagne pieces are much larger in reality than they appear in photographs. They represent the first European portrayal of humans in chess pieces.

The set represents the struggle between the Normans and the Byzantians in the eleventh century, when the Normans had established themselves in southern Italy. The Kings are modeled on Alexius Comnenus and Michael Ducas, leaders in the struggle.

Queens appear for the first time in this set. According to research presented by Russian Grand

Master Yuri Averdakh at the Fifth Biennial meeting of Chess Collectors International in Paris in 1992, the Queens were modeled on two real women: Anna Dassina and Helena. This was not chance; women played prominent roles in Byzantine society.

Another first attributable to the Charlemagne set is the placing of the Kings and Queens on thrones.

Chess certainly reached the British Isles from the Norsemen. One hundred fifty years ago there was a remarkable find on the Isle of Lewis off Scotland that must have come from a Norse shipwreck. The chess pieces found are parts of four sets. The tallest piece is only four and one-eighth inches; all are beautifully made. They have been divided between a museum in Edinburgh and the British Museum.

Curiously, one of the best clues in dating them comes from the Bishop's miter. Ecclesiastical fashions changed, and the Scandinavian carver appears to have copied the latest style of his time, dating the sets to about 1150, according to Michael Taylor of the British Museum.

Nowadays variations in the representation of the Pawn are not as common as they once were. However, their variety has an honorable history dating back to the late thirteenth century when Jacop da Cessole, an Italian Dominican monk, wrote a book of sermons on the subject of chess. Da Cessole describes the Pawns as follows, beginning with the King's Rook and continuing to the Queen's Rook: farm laborer, ferrier, clerk with pen, merchant, physician, tavern keeper, city gate keeper, and gambler.

The advent of American interest in the game in the eighteenth century was commented on by that most versatile of men, Benjamin Franklin, who penned sixteen paragraphs on the "Morals of Chess." He wrote, "Europe has had it over a thousand years; the Spaniards have spread it over their part of America; and it has lately begun its appearance in the United States." Franklin viewed chess as the "most ancient and most universal game known among men; for its original [sic] is beyond the memory of history, and it has, for numberless ages, been the amusement of all the civilized nations of Asia—the Persians, the Indians, and the Chinese."[3]

Thomas Henry Huxley, the nineteenth century English scientist and educator, wrote: "The chess board is the world, the pieces are the phenomena of the universe, the rules of the game are what we call the laws of Nature."[4]

Chess through the ages has tended to hold a fascination for rulers and royal courts, and to be criticized as a waste of time or even banned by some religions. Nonetheless it was a Spanish Catholic bishop, Ruy Lopez, who gave his name to the most famous chess gambit in 1561.

Although enormous scholarly contributions have been made by Russian, German, English, Spanish, Italian, and American researchers, there is no book that brings together the highly complex story of chess sets. (For those who would attempt such a task, a knowledge of Sanskrit might be a prerequisite.)

Chess set collecting also has a long history. The first known collectors were the Urgells of northern Spain.

It has been documented that they owned at least thirteen sets in 1075. In a yet unpublished paper Richard Calvo describes the will of a Count of Urgell written in 1010, donating a chess set to the monastery of St. Giles.

Dr. Calvo has carefully investigated the provenance of three of the Urgell chess sets made of stunning crystal with hard-stone carving that traces to Fatimite Egypt. In 1070 there were ninety-six pieces. Five hundred years later there were only forty-four. In 1887 fourteen pieces were documented. These were in the private collection of a French Countess, Mme. de Bahague, in 1907. A few years ago they appeared at a French auction and were purchased by the Emir of Kuwait for his National Museum.

The pieces apparently became part of the chessboard maneuvers of the Middle East because, after the Iraqi invasion, they appeared in Baghdad, and when the Gulf War ended they were moved again— back to Kuwait.

It is rare for the ordinary collector to find pieces of such antiquity—or to be able to afford them—but one never gives up hope. Gareth and Vel Williams, the doyens of British collectors, once had the sharp eyes and expertise to pick up a ninth century Persian chess piece at an auction of Middle East artifacts. Perhaps the most magnificent set ever made in Koenigsburg (now Kaliningrad, Russia)—made of amber and dated 1616—sold at auction in 1990 for more than $500,000.

Chess set collectors have been organized as a group for only a decade, starting with a meeting arranged by Dr. George Dean, a Michigan physician. Some collectors are erudite about the game and the business of collecting sets. There are at least five hundred serious collectors known to the organization, Chess Collectors International. The majority are in four countries: Germany, England, Russia, and the United States. Also represented are Japan, Italy, India, and France. Bonds have developed among collectors; they are strengthened through regular distribution of a newsletter and at biennial meetings.

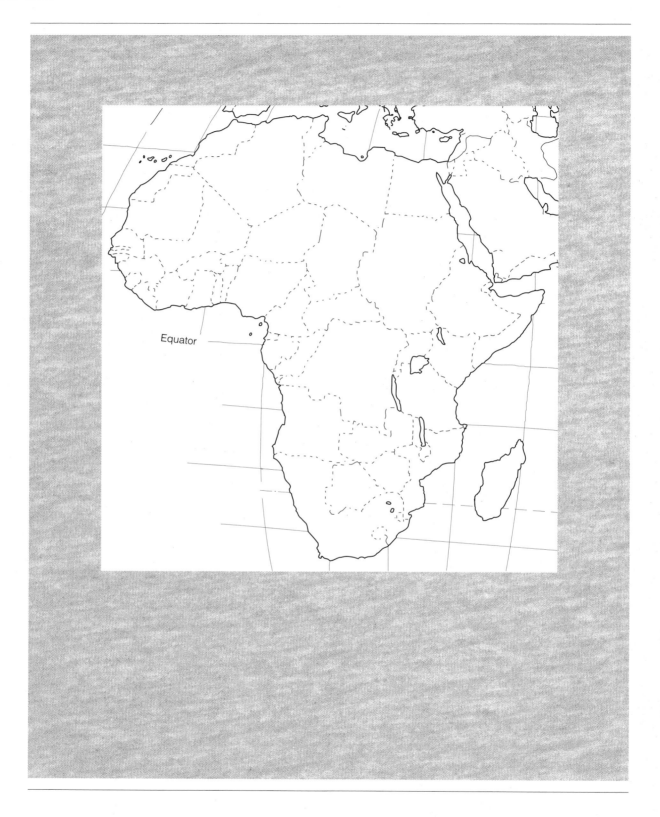

Equator

INTRODUCTION TO VOLUME 1: SUB-SAHARAN AFRICA

Almost all the great art and artifacts of sub-Saharan Africa are in European and American museums. Many artifacts do not survive fifty years in the African climate; others are destroyed for cultural reasons. Most of sub-Saharan Africa does not have a long history of chess sets. But I believe there were sets in tropical Africa in the nineteenth century. A history of chess in southern Africa, coinciding with the migration of Dutch, British, Portuguese, and Malay over the centuries, is a subject that calls for extensive research.

Time may reveal more than we know today. I expect that some of the greatest archaeological discoveries of the twenty-first century will be in northeast Africa, possibly centered on the little-known Meroe civilization well south of the great Egyptian discoveries.

This introduction will consider three distinct chess sets that relate to the history of pre-colonial sub-Saharan Africa: the Ubar set; the Welled Selasse set from Ethiopia; and the set from Bornu, Nigeria.

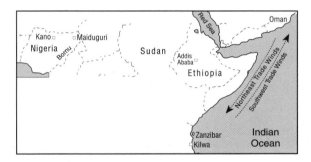

THE UBAR SET

In the 1980s George Hedges—an attorney by profession but an archaeologist at heart, with a graduate degree in that field—and some of my colleagues at the Jet Propulsion Laboratory, which is managed by Caltech, began looking for the ancient city of Ubar,

described in the Old Testament and storied in the Koran and The Arabian Nights. Ubar was a major stop on the long-lost frankincense trail across the empty quarter of Arabia.

Satellite cameras, originally designed for detecting Soviet missile sites under many feet of earth, worked beautifully in finding traces of moisture under the dry Arabian desert from one hundred miles up. The last successful Challenger mission produced photographs that traced an ancient river bed across Oman.

After Hedges, who speaks passable Arabic, received the blessing of the Sultan of Oman, he and other members of the team, including Nicholas Clapp, an ex-National Geographic photographer, and Juris Zarins, an archaeology professor at Southwest Missouri University, were given the use of the Royal Omani Air Force helicopters to reach promising sites. Eventually, the lost city of Ubar was found.

Then, in 1993, at a new excavation bordering the biblical frankincense route in Oman, a team of Middle East experts discovered a chess set *in situ*. Zarins, a member of the team, wrote to me that "six pieces were found together in the trash in the central western tower. One piece was found burned in the southeast corner room of the main wall. I suggest a date of tenth century A.D." Some published references to the pieces questioned their composition. Zarins assured me that they are all sandstone.

An archaeological dig in Oman may seem a strange approach to sub-Saharan chess sets—unless you have sat, as I have, on the palm-girted shores of Zanzibar, almost overcome by the pungent odor of cloves, watching the dhows from Oman arrive on the monsoon winds. These annual arrivals stretch back at least two thousand years.[1]

The rise of Islam after the prophet Mohammed's birth in 571 stimulated emigration. Shiite refugees from Oman arrived in Zanzibar in the seventh century when the Omanis were already busy using Zanzibar as the trading entrepôt of the whole East African coast. The Portuguese came to be the dominant power from 1503 until 1698, when the Omanis captured the key fort of Mombasa in what is now Kenya. There were various shifting alliances of power, but by 1832 Seyyid Saud bin Sultan, who had been elected to the imamate in 1804, was in full control.

He moved his capital from Muscat, in Oman, to Zanzibar. The Sultan introduced cloves from the Moluccas and laid the basis of Zanzibar's agricultural riches. Not until 1861 did Zanzibar become independent of Oman. By 1890 the Sultan of Zanzibar placed his country under formal British rule. But the trade between Oman and Zanzibar, borne by the steady monsoons that alternate every six months, continues

Ubar Chess Set, c. 950 A.D.

to this day. When I first visited Zanzibar in 1950, the Sultan and his court were still closely intermarried with Omani royalty.

So the Omanis were vital factors in Zanzibar for a thousand years. Their cultural influence remains strong even now, despite that day in 1964 when some twenty thousand Arabs were gathered in the football stadium and slaughtered by the black Africans they had long oppressed.

I have to believe that over the centuries Omani traders carried more than a few chess sets with them to occupy their time at sea and, thus, introduced chess to the eastern part of Africa. (Michael Mark, the *fundi* [real expert, in Kiswahili] on Indian chess sets, raises the possibility that the centuries old trading in ivory between Africa and India might well have included chess sets.) The idea that Omani dhows carried chess sets to Zanzibar at an early period has a measure of supporting evidence in the discovery by the Institute of Nautical Archaeology of a shipwreck at Serce Liman on the Turkish coast opposite Rhodes. Although this disaster occurred in an entirely different direction from Zanzibar, it does illustrate that chess sets were carried on ships in this early period. From the coins and the glass weights that were used to weigh them, the so-called glass shipwreck was closely dated to between 1021 and 1025. Eight wooden chess pieces, similar to those found at Ubar, were taken from the shipwreck. They are crudely carved abstract shapes used to represent kings, elephants, horses, and other chess pieces.

I predict that, when the cultural fabric of the east coast is better known, one patch in the quilt will be chess pieces. Ancient chess sets will be found, I believe, when the current political turmoil ceases, allowing careful archaeological research under the stone buildings built centuries ago. I've walked the crooked alleys in Zanzibar's Old Town, marveling at the carved wooden doors and their metal studs, so magnificent and striking that their export is specifically forbidden. How I longed to explore the succession of hearths to be found in those houses of antiquity.

As Randall Pouwels says in his study of Islam on the East African coast from 1800 to 1900: "I am aware that there are valuable privately owned materials, such as diaries, in the possession of various individuals and families in Mombasa, Lamu, and Zanzibar. Few such individuals are willing to allow researchers to examine these treasures."[2] This reticence is likely to apply to family artifacts such as chess sets.

For good luck, Basil Davidson, the brilliant British historian of Africa, once gave me a ninth century coin dug up at Kilwa, a famous east coast site. Perhaps it will bring me a chess set from the ancient port of Zanzibar.

THE WELLED SELASSE SET

Looking more widely across sub-Saharan Africa, the doyen of chess scholars, H. J. R. Murray says: "I have been unable to discover any evidence for the practice of chess in Equatorial or Southern Africa, or even in Muhammedan Western Africa."[3]

However, Murray does point to Henry Salt, an Englishman who traveled in Ethiopia from 1802 to 1806, as the man who brought back to Europe the chess set of Welled Selasse, the Ras of Tigre. Salt recalled with a certain irony that everyone—even the slaves—gave advice to the chess players, but somehow the ras or king always won. An interesting footnote is that W. C. Plowden, who was the British consul from 1843 to 1847, found that chess was one of the main subjects in the education of a Tigrean chief. Plowden writes that the people of Tigre were much more interested in chess than the Amharas, who have dominated Ethiopia in the last century.[4]

Welled Selasse's chess set may be seen by scholars on appointment in the Museum of Mankind, which is part of the British Museum. The light brown set, reproduced here in black and white, is essentially a series of cylindrical pieces, which may suggest a Muslim influence. Murray shows other Tigre pieces that also lack any figural hints.

Emperor Haile Selassie once told the British scholar Richard Pankhurst that he recalled chess boards used by the courtiers in Addis Ababa as well as

Welled Selasse Chess Set, 18th Century

in provincial capitals. Haile Selassie also said that, in the reign of Menelik II (1844-1923), Empress Taytu was devoted to chess.

It was my privilege to have several audiences with Haile Selassie in Addis Ababa. In 1950 he generously gave me a silver Coptic cross. If only I'd had the nerve to suggest a chess set instead.

Going further back than Salt, there is an account from 1524 of a Venetian scholar, Alessandro Zorzi, who learned that Emperor Lebna Dengel played chess.[5]

The mountains of Ethiopia and the desert to the south have left the Amharic Ethiopians on a Christian Coptic island in a Muslim sea. Ethiopian chess sets will be discussed and illustrated in another volume of this series.

THE BORNU SET

In 1925 the British anthropologist C. K. Meek brought three chess sets from Bornu, Nigeria. According to Michael Mark, the always well-informed former editor of The Chess Collector, one is in the British Museum of Mankind;[6] another, in the New

York Metropolitan; the third, in Grandmaster Lothar Schmidt's collection in Germany.[7] In a brief article in the March, 1934 issue of *Man*, Meek wrote that he observed a game using conventional chess moves, but that players could disrupt their opponents' concentration by interjections such as "kus-kus-kus-kus." The photograph accompanying that article shows an unusual feature of the set: a general (*kaigama*) is used

Bornu Chess Set

for a lesser piece, the Castle.[8] Sir Richard Palmer described the kaigama as a ruler in the south. Palmer quotes from a long poem illustrating the lesser position: "If the Sultan counts as ten large whole kolanuts, the Kaigama counts as twenty halves."[9]

Meek reported that the game played among the Kanuri people in the old Bornu capital of Birni Ngsar Gomo was named Tsatsarandi, a word he finds similar to Shatranj, a name for chess from the Middle East.

The British collector Gareth Williams gave me a photograph showing Kanuri players in Maiduguri in 1930. Williams said the game was played on a leather board fringed with lace used to tie it up when rolled. Players followed the rules of "Shatrans" or pre-fifteenth-century Europe; opponents were allowed to distract each other by reciting verses of the Koran.

Meek's Bornu set in the Metropolitan is from the Gustav Pfeiffer collection. Curator Jessie McNab describes it as made from whittled limba wood, singed for the dark side. The King and Queen are similar, the King being distinguished by a robe of blue striped cotton. The pieces show strong Islamic influence. The long "ears" of the Castle are an exaggeration of an early form that McNab ascribes to Persia (Nishapur) in the early ninth century.[10]

This set clearly suggests the movement of chess from the Middle East or the Arabian peninsula westward to northern Nigeria, rather than coming up from the south with the colonial conquest. The Bornu Empire began about the year 1000, according to Palmer, and continued for eight centuries until about 1808. It can be surmised that chess, along with the horse, the camel, and papyrus boats (on the Nile to Lake Chad), made a westward migration that swam with the Muslim tide over the centuries. Meek's Bornu chess set is, I am convinced, a successor to many sets copied and modified over a period of at least a thousand years.

Ignorance of the history of this part of Africa during the Middle Ages is a lacuna in western scholarship. It has its roots in malice against the spread of Islam, especially after the Christian Nubians embraced the Prophet. It has been argued that, to justify the slave trade, there was a need to consciously or unconsciously deprive Africans, such as the Nigerians in Bornu, of a cultural history and even full humanity. The discovery of the chimpanzee and the gorilla in Africa was linked to blacks to indicate a sub-human status.[11]

Ignorance and prejudice toward Africa in the Middle Ages is one reason for the racist and stereotypical representation of Africans in some chess sets such as the "African-European" set described on page 45 in this book.

And the problem is not restricted to the Middle Ages. It is hard to overestimate the cultural arrogance that Europeans of the nineteenth century displayed toward African history. Dr. Ekpo Eyo, the Nigerian scholar and former conservator of the National Museum in Lagos, has done the most to blow away this miasma of ignorance and misinformation. Dr. Eyo questions the assertion by early European experts, including the great German explorer and anthropologist Frobenius, that some of the most magnificent early Nigerian bronzes must have been made by a long lost group of wandering Greek artists. Eyo has proven that the Nigerian pieces antedate the comparable Greek bronzes. Would it not be logical to reverse the conclusion and suggest, as jocular Eyo does, that perhaps the spectacular Greek bronzes were made by a lost tribe of Nigerians?[12]

It should be emphasized that there are copious documents, such as *The Kano Chronicle*,[13] that allow the period to be delineated. Even more has been published about art during the Neolithic in the Sahara. However, it seems that, compared to kings and battles, games lack historians.

A game with roots in a fire cult that extends back to southern Arabia is in existence among the Tuareg in the Sahara. It involves placing a boulder, the bigger the better, on top of a trilith of inscribed stones made into a crude hearth.

When I hitchhiked across the Sahara from Algiers to the Tuareg oasis of Tamanrasset in 1960, I wasn't wise enough to observe their games. But games existed and surely chess was one. Maiduguri, an old capital of Bornu, is a source of manuscripts less famous but as informative as *The Kano Chronicle*. How vividly I recall walking the dusty street of Maiduguri in the 1950s. Unfortunately, at the time I was oblivious of the great wealth of knowledge that exists in Arabic and other sources about the events and customs, the great battles, the droughts, the continual flood of peoples of diverse stock across the region. On Maiduguri's ancient streets I passed many houses that seemed to pre-exist time. But I was too young, too ignorant, and too naive to grasp the great stability and continuity of the Bornu people.

Yet my ignorance was not greater than that of Trevor Roper, the Oxford professor who made a fool of himself in the 1950s by saying that no history existed for this part of Africa or sub-Saharan Africa in general. The page on Bornu from the King Charles V Catalan Atlas of 1375 gave Charles more knowledge of Bornu than Professor Roper or me.

Another distinct possibility regarding the origin of chess in Africa deserves mention. The Portuguese, coming from the south, may have brought chess to southern Nigeria in the sixteenth century. There are many so-called Portuguese ivories, with European faces, that were made by Africans. I have never seen such an ivory that cried out "I am a chess piece." But there may well be a complete set in the bottom basement of some Portuguese museum or at one of the Yoruba courts.

So I conclude that we lack knowledge of chess in the whole Islamic belt crossing east to west, south of the Sahara, only because we haven't found it yet. Oh, to be back in Timbuktu when its library possibly had more books than any in Europe. Chess must have been there.

Today, despite a lessening of prejudice and an increase in scholarship on Africa, our ignorance continues because, as one of Basil Davidson's favorite Chinese phrases puts it, "We are looking at flowers from horseback." ▣

PART ONE

EASTERN AFRICA

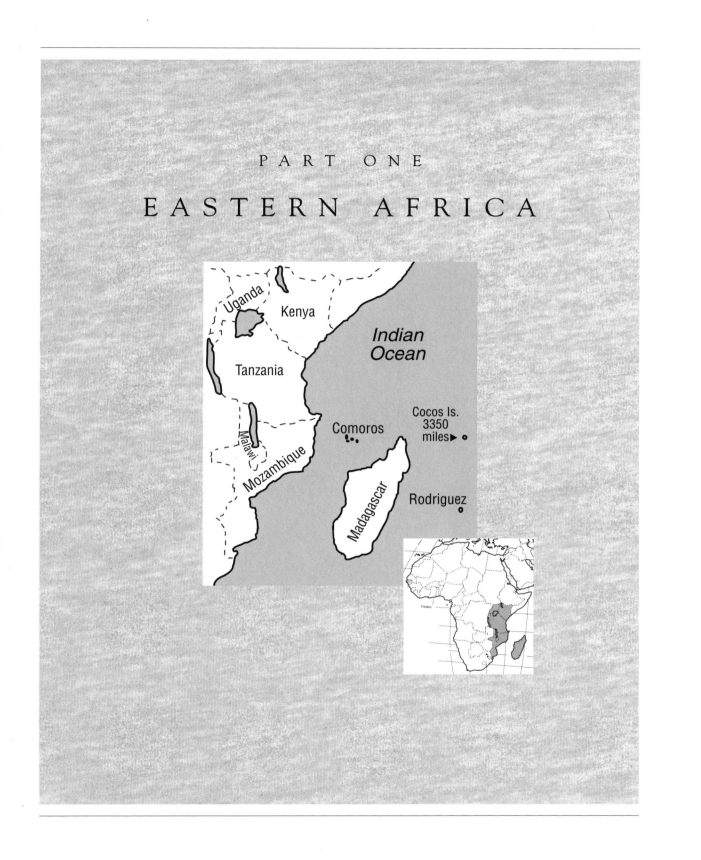

UGANDA

THE KABAKA, THEN AND NOW

Figures 1a and 1b • Ceramic

Kabaka Frederick Mutesa (King Freddie in the British tabloids) stood next to me at a cocktail party held for the cast and producers of the MGM film *King Solomon's Mines* and nodded toward a beautiful, freckle-faced, auburn-haired woman in the crowd, confiding, "I'd like her tonight." Taking a deep breath, I replied to the king's arrogance: "Well, Your Majesty, I think you'd best speak to Lieutenant Colonel Bartley, her husband. He's that tall chap next to her."

That memory flooded back to me during the 1994 Academy Awards when Deborah Kerr received a standing ovation and an honorary Oscar for lifetime achievement. It was this lovely British actress who had attracted His Majesty's lascivious interest at that party on Makerere Hill in Kampala, Uganda in 1950, during an era when the farther you were from London, the more elaborately you dressed. The king's suit sported a swath of royal leopard skin draped elaborately over the shoulder. But Deborah Kerr and her co-star, Stewart Grainger, shocked the little colonial society by wearing simple tourist khaki.

Uganda is a bastardization of *Buganda*, dropping the B and using the Kiswahili U (for country) combined with the root *ganda*. Buganda is one of four kingdoms that formed a part of Uganda. It is the kingdom of the Baganda, a Bantu-speaking African people. *Muganda* is an individual. *Kiganda* stands for customs. *Luganda* is the language. Kiswahili is the correct term for Swahili.

Buganda had a magical quality about it when the first Europeans arrived in the late nineteenth century. Later, Sir Winston Churchill described the feeling of climbing up a rope like Jack's beanstalk and arriving in Buganda, "the pearl of Africa."

Indeed, the small kingdom had good roads, a well-established system of government, land registration, a kingly hierarchy, and a well-developed set of religious customs. A Muganda could feed a family of four by tending his plantains for six weeks or so annually. It is no wonder that the British government seriously contemplated settling the Jewish population of the diaspora in Buganda rather than in Palestine after World War I. Buganda was a far more fertile land. (Of course, in considering that plan, not much thought was given to the rights of the indigenous Baganda.)

A great deal of Buganda history is covered in an earlier book,[1] so I will be brief here. The British did not colonize, but established a protectorate in 1894; it included Buganda, three associated small kingdoms, and a number of Nilotic ethnic groups from the north—to make a country.[2]

Uganda had such potential for becoming a prosperous democracy. The year I lived at Makerere University (1950) to research my doctoral thesis, there was much hope for the country. Its red murram (clay) roads were well maintained. It had the railroad from Mombasa and the flying boat on Lake Victoria on the route to Southampton. Electricity was provided by a dam where Lake Victoria spilled over to form part of the white Nile. In addition to the ample foodstuffs of plantains and other tropical fruits, it had valuable coffee, cotton, tea, sugar cane, and even profitable copper ore reserves. The population was by far the best educated in eastern or central Africa. Uganda had more African college graduates than Kenya, Tanzania, Northern Rhodesia, Southern Rhodesia, and Nyasaland combined. It also had the best medical school between Egypt and South Africa. There were great possibilities for tourism.

Then • King

Now • Bishop

As independence approached in 1962, Kabaka Frederick Mutesa was unwilling to accept a subordinate position to the "less cultured" national leader elected from the northwest. The confrontation between the kabaka and President Obote ended with the government troops, led by a young and ambitious Idi Amin, storming the Lubiri, Mutesa's compound, while he escaped in woman's clothing, eventually making his way to England. He never had dinner with Miss Kerr. He died in the U.K. of alcoholism, while still a relatively young man.

Long years of internecine war during the 1970s left the Baganda devastated. Idi Amin ruled as president from 1971 until his exile in 1979. He was Africa's worst, murdering tyrant. This was a long way from the days when he was a bellboy at a Kampala hotel.

What Amin didn't ruin, AIDS has decimated. Years before the term was known in America the Baganda were well aware of whole villages of orphans whose parents had died of the "wasting disease."

Fortunately, my Baganda godchildren (three sets of twins from the same parents) are healthy and living in the United States. All have American graduate degrees. Their father, Senteza Kajubi, whom I brought to the University of Chicago for a graduate degree, has retired as vice chancellor of Makerere University.

You can tell that I have a deep emotional commitment to Uganda. I was delighted to acquire a chess set representing it. The artist was Margaret Robinson (an African American whom you will read more about later in the description of the Benin set). Reverend Sams Kironde-Kogozi,[3] founder of the Christian University of East Africa, arranged for the design and checked it.

The set portrays two periods in the life of the Baganda, as interpreted for me by Reverend Sams. One side depicts traditional life circa 1890, at the time the British arrived; the other, modern Baganda life in 1993. That was the year President Museveni, who is not a Muganda, restored the monarchy, with ceremonial powers only, in a move to touch a chord in the Baganda and build political capital.

On the traditional side the King is a kabaka wearing the leopard skin restricted to royalty. The Queen is Nalinnya, the kabaka's sister and lubuga (co-heir). The Bishop represents a traditional healer, with a gourd in each hand; the Knight, a warrior with woven shield and spear. The king's official residence, Twekobe, is the Castle. The reed enclosure comes down to the ground except at the entrance. The Pawns wear traditional bark cloth attire; it was made from the inner bark of certain trees, which was soaked and beaten to create a textile-like material.

On the modern side the King represents the kabaka today. The Queen is Naunya, his sister and co-heir. The Bishop is an Anglican carrying a typical crook; the Knight, a soldier of today bearing an automatic weapon. The Castle represents the modern parliament building. The Pawns wear modern male attire.

Long after I commissioned the Buganda set in 1993, I heard from my friend William Kalema, Ph.D.,[4] financial advisor to the kabaka, that the newly installed king, Ronald Mutebi II, was coming to Los Angeles.

Mutebi attended primary school in Buganda and then grew up in England, which accounts for his impeccable upper-class English accent. When I first met his father, Kabaka Mutesa, a principal subject for gossip was the way he seemed to alternate evenings between his wife, Queen Damali, and her twin sister

Sarah. Kabaka Mutebi is Sarah's son. The queen did have a son, Henry, with Mutesa's brother. Henry was an unsuccessful claimant for the kabakaship.

Mutebi was crowned in 1993, the thirty-sixth kabaka in a line stretching back almost seven hundred years to 1314 A.D.

He was the first kabaka to make an official visit to the United States. I was fortunate to attend the royal ball held in his honor in Los Angeles, along with hundreds of Baganda, many in traditional dress. The local Uganda community had arranged to give His Royal Highness a white- and gold-trimmed copy of my chess set. It was presented to the kabaka by the artist, Margaret Robinson, who said the occasion was one of the highlights of her life. Unlike some of her less polite fellow Americans, Robinson bowed when she was presented to the kabaka. Later she told me she was thinking: "I've had to kiss a lot of white behinds in my life; I can certainly bow to a black king."

KENYA
LUO
Figure 2 • Kisii Stone

Southern Kenya may have been home to the first humans on earth about two million years ago, according to anthropological discoveries. The Luo of western Kenya are a delightful Nilotic people who have engaged in an unsuccessful contest with the Kikuyu and the Kalenjin for control of their country since its independence in 1963.

Kisii is a market town just east of Lake Victoria. Chess sets from the region usually display the natural white and pink of Kisii stone. This blue and red set, made from white stone, was stained by the carver.

Collectors have asked me about the King's huge, elongated headdress. Luo warriors wear this *ogudi* tradi-

tionally, covered with animal skins. The other exceptional feature of this set is the disproportionate height of the Pawns. They are actually taller than the Castles.

Thousands of such sets have been made in East Africa. Over the years there has been a marked uniformity in the style of the sets despite variations in size and color. The price also varies: the farther from the source, the more expensive the set.

KENYA
ANIMALS
Figure 3 • Kisii Stone

This animal set of unstained, extremely frangible, soft stone was introduced, as far as I can tell, in about 1989. The lion is King, with a crown that comes close to being a dunce cap. A stately giraffe is Queen. The Bishops are rhinos. (I have known a few bishops who had short horns, were shortsighted, and made a ferocious sound.) The Knights are antelopes; the Castles, elephants. Surprisingly, the Pawns are people.

TANZANIA
MAASAI
Figure 4 • Wood

As befits my favorite African animal, the giraffe as Knight is taller than the King and Queen. The Queen's large necklace and the beehive hut as Castle are characteristically Maasai.

The Bishop is a *sangoma*. Pejoratively but inaccurately known in the western world as witch doctors, sangomas might more correctly be compared to shamans or medicine men. They are believed to have supernatural powers of healing and divination.

A most colorful East African ethnic group, the Maasai are divided between southern Kenya and northern Tanzania. They are a Nilotic people, a grouping

Luo • Knight

King

Queen

that differs from the Bantu-speaking majority. Like many pastoral Nilotic peoples who exalt the warrior class, the Maasai have been far less influenced by westerners than their Bantu brothers, such as the Kikuyu.

This unique set was carved for me in Nanyuki, the town known to most travelers to eastern Africa as "near the Mount Kenya Safari Club." I am grateful to Lucy Githinji, manager of the club's gift shop, for designing the set and pursuing a carver on my behalf. I first entered into conversation with her because she has the same surname as one of my best Kikuyu friends, Dr. Philip Githinji.[5]

TANZANIA
A Set As Yet Unrealized

The challenge of creating a sense of national unity among the various ethnic groups in his country was very much on the mind of Julius Nyerere in 1958, the year before he became Prime Minister of Tanganyika. Nationalism in both Kenya and Tanzania was necessary in the struggle against British colonialism. Unity was so important that Nyrerere delayed Tanzania's independence for a year, hoping that the East African Federation could be maintained. In 1964 he became his country's first president.

Nyerere and I had just taped a radio discussion at the NBC studio on Michigan Avenue one day in 1958, and he was to stay with me in my apartment at the University of Chicago. He asked how we would get there, and I said we'd take the Illinois Central because I didn't own a car. Nyerere, known for his long walks and his walking stick, asked me how far it was.

"Oh, about ten miles," I said, not grasping his point.

Nyerere said, "You know, Ned, I think best when I walk, and I haven't been able to walk much on this visit to America. Can't we walk?"

So we set off down Michigan Avenue and onto South Park Way, through what was then the affluent black South Side. We stopped at the offices of *Ebony*. Nyerere, as the leader of the independence forces against British colonialism in Tanzania, was warmly welcomed by publisher John Johnson and his staff.

Walking again, Nyerere wrestled aloud with what measures could be used to bind the disparate elements in his nation, once a German protectorate and then a British mandate. One idea he mentioned was scheduling more national football games. (Once, at a league championship game in Dar-es-Salaam, Nyerere invited me to kick out the first ball.)

Talking with other Tanzanians and Kenyan leaders such as Tom Mboya in later years, I approached the unity question by asking what national, rather than ethnic or tribal, icons they would use to represent their countries in a chess set.

Chess set aficionados agreed that Kenya's sacred Mount Kenya and Tanzania's Mount Kilimanjaro (the mountain of the spirit Njaro) would be the Castles. Kilimanjaro is of course the highest mountain in Africa, at almost twenty thousand feet. Map students will know there is a jag in the border dividing Kenya and Tanzania; it delineates what used to be German territory—a gift from Queen Victoria to her cousin Kaiser Wilhelm—and includes Kilimanjaro. Early geographers in London believed the silver cap of Kibo peak was salt; they thought it could not be snow because of the mountain's proximity to the equator.

When I was in Moshi, at the foot of the mountain, to write an article on the Chagga, who grow coffee on the slopes of Kilimanjaro, Tanzanians there agreed it should be the Castle.

I did fulfill a dream in climbing to the top. It is not dangerous for fit people. Yes, climbing three steps and slipping back two over the scree or cinders is exhausting. But at least half the climbers overcome altitude sickness and fatigue to reach the top. The great secret lies in the Kiswahili words *pole, pole* (slowly, slowly). If you move fast even over fairly level ground you may well collapse.

Ernest Hemingway and other writers have created great mystery around the remains of a leopard found on top of Kibo peak. How did it get there? Why, in some spiritual sense, did it climb so far to die? I never saw the remains, but they are clear in my mind. That leopard must be the Knight in my Tanzanian set.

Sangomas are the obvious choice for Bishops. The psychiatrist I saw function most successfully with black Africans worked in Sukumaland in Tanzania. What could one highly trained mental health specialist do for three million people? His answer was to form a health network with the sangomas. He cleverly figured out what emotional and "Dear Abby" types of problems they could best handle and particularly enlisted their help with illnesses that invoked fears of spells, with which British-trained doctors have no experience or power. By working with the people and not fighting their ways, he broke the tradition of a straitjacketed western approach to mental health that had been practiced by the first generation of British-trained psychiatrists. With his system, the people who would most benefit from western techniques, drugs, or even hospitalization could be filtered up the network to the western-trained doctor.

Ideas for the other chess pieces came from sitting around campfires. All the Kikuyu I talked to wanted Kenyatta for King on the Kenya side. Nyerere was the favored choice for the Tanzanian King. One day I may yet realize a chess set that represents national unity in the two countries.

MALAWI
Figure 5 • Wood

In Malawi there are four main centers where chess sets are carved. All are in the southern part of the country, and all the carvers are of Yao extraction. Although Yaos are Muslim, they have no problem with the representation of human figures in their chess sets, unlike carvers from other Islamic countries.

The first center is in the village of Chingali, on the other side of the mountain from the old colonial capital of Zomba. The extended Jibu family, comprising about forty people, makes the chess sets from ebony *mphingo* wood and light *kadale* wood.

The second carving center is at Liwonde, above the last cataract on the Shire River before it enters Lake Malombe. Here the Daudi family makes chess sets from mphingo and either the light *mpasa* or the red *bwemba* wood.

The third is at Mulanje, near the Church of Central Africa Presbyterian mission on the road to Likabula Pools on beautiful Mt. Mulanji. The sets are produced by the Masauli family from dark *msumwa* and light *mkomwa* wood.

The fourth center is near Salima. Here the woods used are mphingo for the dark side and mkomwa for the light.

Malachite sets, brought in from Zaire, can also be found in Malawi. Reasonably sized malachite sets are rare because of the brittleness of the material. For the light sides of the malachite sets, hippo ivory—instead of elephant ivory—is used because of international customs concerns.[6]

Queen

I have known 96-year-old Kamuzu Banda, the former president of Malawi, for over forty years, and met with him in his country as well as in London and Ghana. Once, in 1957, we were on our hands and knees in his presidential office looking at a map he had spread out. He showed me what he claimed to be the extent of the old Maravi empire, which included parts of present-day Zambia, Tanzania, and Mozambique. I suggested a chess set could be designed to represent the people who lived in that territory five hundred years ago. He liked the idea, although I rather think he also wanted me to design a contemporary set, with him as King.

Bone • Knight

As we discussed the historical set, it became clear that, because he is pro-western, he did not want Europeans as the antagonists. He wanted Arabs! Most Africans have forgotten that Malawi had been one of the areas raided by slavers based on Zanzibar, who sent their human cargoes to Oman and Arabia—not to the Americas. As a result of that slave trading, President Banda had an intense hatred of Arabs—so intense that he antagonized the Muslims in the north of his country, even though they are of the same Bantu stock as his Chichewa-speaking people. Nonetheless, I think Banda recognized in his mirror some Arab ancestry, which I found reflected in his physiognomy.[7]

Serpentine • King

Later, while Banda and I were discussing the design of a modern Malawi chess set, it occurred to me that Reverend Chilembwe, the American-educated Malawian preacher, might be a good model for the Bishop. Carelessly, I asked Banda how old he had been at the time of Chilembwe's uprising in 1913. Banda got a cunning look on his face, as though he thought I was trying to trap him into revealing his age. He

abruptly ended our discussion of both chess sets and said his driver was waiting for me. So expired that idea.

The new president of Malawi is a Yao, like the carver of this rather crude set. The Castles are slender huts; the Knights, horses; the Bishops, thick-lipped.

MALAWI

Figure 6 • Ebony and Red-painted Bone

The style of this set is similar to the previous one, but the carving is superior. The Knight is a highly stylized elephant. The Bishop is a woman pounding mealies (corn) to make *posho,* a traditional dish. The Pawns hold an unidentified object in their left hands and a broad sword in their right. The shape of the sword is more Arab than African.

MALAWI

Figure 7 & Cover • Black and Green Serpentine

Malawians are the pre-eminent carvers in southern and eastern Africa and do show up in all the major cities. If you look for a carver in Cape Town, you are most likely to find a Malawian. I suspect that this particular set was made by a Malawi carver in Zimbabwe, where there is more work in serpentine than in the special carving villages of Malawi described earlier. The style of this set follows that of the much more common Malawi wooden sets, but has superior detail.

When Malawi's deputy minister of education, Mrs. Chipembere, visited me, she was surprised to see so many Malawi sets in my office. She had been unaware that such a flourishing small-scale business in Malawian chess sets existed.

She was accompanied by her youngest son, who was born in Los Angeles while his parents were in exile. Masouka, which means "suffering," listened avidly as we discussed the old days in Malawi and the fight against the British-imposed Federation of Rhodesia and Nyasaland.

It is almost certainly true that Henry Chipembere would have succeeded Kamuzu Banda as president of Malawi. But as Banda once said to me in his office, "Ned, when you see Chip in Los Angeles again, tell him that if he comes back here he will be eaten by crocodiles."

Chip died of diabetes when Masouka was only four, so the son had no memory of his father's voice. When I played the two-hour tape of my 1976 interview with Chipembere, it was a rare emotional experience for Masouka.

Chipembere was a wise and kind man. I'd like to think that the Kings in this set catch something of his visage.

MALAWI

Figure 8 and Cover • Ebony and Red Wood

Output from the chess-set-making villages in Malawi shows minor variations in style. In this set, for example, the features are much sharper than in the others in my collection. All the pieces, including the Pawns, are carved with precision and obvious workmanship.

MADAGASCAR

MERINA VS. SAKALAVA

Figure 9 • Cattle Horn

Madagascar is the second largest island in the world. Its inhabitants are known as Malagasy. The white side of this Malagasy set represents the Merina people of the highland around Tananarive. They migrated from Java in the eighth, eleventh, and fourteenth centuries, and one can see something of their Malay features.

The black side represents the Sakalava people around Majunga, with their more African features.

The white King is modeled on the nineteenth-century Merina ruler, King Radama. (In my African manuscript collection there are letters in both French and English signed by Radama.) The Queen is characteristic of the Merina nobility. The Bishop is portrayed as a letter carrier. The Zebu cow is a distinctive Knight. The Castle represents the palace in Tananarive. The Pawns are soldiers equipped with nineteenth-century French rifles and bayonets.

The black Knights and Bishops are the same as the white, but are thicker lipped to represent the Sakalava. African features are also evident in the King and Queen. The Castle is an *antandroy* statue. Malagasy carve them in wood for grave markers. The birds are frequently found on posts at the four corners of the graves. However, this practice may be borrowed from the Merina culture. The Pawns, wearing loincloths, carry spears and shields.

The French curator of the National Museum, who sold me this set in 1951, estimated that it had been made in about 1875. He had decided not to keep it because chess was not a traditional Malagasy game. Today the Malagasy have become far more aware of their culture, and traditional artifacts are rarely available for legal export. I doubt that anything over one hundred years old would be licensed for sale now.

MADAGASCAR

MERINA

Figure 10 • Wood

Forty years after buying the first Madagascar set, I purchased this one which was made around 1980.

Both sides are the same design and represent the dominant, present-day Merina peoples of the high-

Merina • Queen

Ebony • King

Bishop

lands. The King is dressed as a typical Merina man, in a long coat. (In real life the coat would have a slit for easier movement.) The Queen is a Merina lady with umbrella. Her hair is correctly braided. The shawl over her right shoulder indicates that she is single; if it were draped over the left, it would mean she was married. The Knight is the ubiquitous Zebu humped cattle. The Castles are traditional Merina royalty burial houses (*tranovola*).

There is no religious significance to the Bishop's attire. In fact, the dress is more coastal and non-Merina, since the brimless cap and short pants are worn only by small boys in the highland areas, where the nights are quite cold. The Pawns are warriors, but of the nineteenth century and not the sort seen today. These anomalies point up the fact that most ethnic chess sets are not anthropologically correct.

These errors would, I knew, be noticed by my colleague Murray Gell-Mann when he came to see my two Madagascar sets. A New York Times article on May 4, 1994, celebrating the publication of Gell-Mann's book *The Quark and the Jaguar*, describes him as "the man who knows everything." I've met thousands of people smarter than I, but have had more proof from Gell-Mann than from anyone else.

We first met in 1951, eight years before he won the Nobel Prize in physics, but long after his friends were awed by his devouring search for knowledge. I take some pride in having asked him to become a trustee of the Leakey Foundation. Despite his ever-present impatience with lesser humans, he was quite enthusiastic about lesser primates and made seminal contributions to the study of lemurs and the protection of their habitat.

One of his many facets is a gift for languages. He once sent me a telegram in Kiswahili that was far too erudite for the up-country Swahili I learned in Uganda. When I disposed of my library on sub-Saharan Africa, I gave Gell-Mann first choice on the African dictionaries and grammar books. He bought close to one hundred volumes, including several on Malagasy languages.

I'm not sure if the dictionaries or our discussion about my Madagascar chess sets influenced his decision, but he was soon off to "the great red island" for a month to look at everything, as is his wont. Some of his interest arose from his being a trustee of the MacArthur Foundation, which was involved with conservation.

On his return from the land of lemurs, he presented a brilliant two-hour lecture for my student seminar. He expounded on Malagasy history and its flora and fauna. He described the island's present state as an ecological disaster area, ninety percent deforested, its lifeblood of red soil staining the rivers crimson as they run to the sea. (When he reads this, Gell-Mann will probably think of several rivers that do not carry excessive sediment; my hyperbole shows I'm not the precise scientist he has remained during the forty-plus years we've been colleagues.)

Chess sets are almost too modern for his taste, which runs more to pre-Columbian artifacts (although he does have a fabulous collection of Native American rugs). As we discussed this Madagascar set, Gell-Mann compared the Castle to the posts that stand in the four corners of a Malagasy grave. He also noted the absence of lemurs, which might have served as the Knights.

One day after I had published a chapter of anecdotes about another colleague and Nobel Laureate,

Richard Feynman, Gell-Mann—who is as different from his competitor Feynman as chalk is from cheese—accosted me on the Caltech campus and demanded to know, "Why did you write about that creep Feynman, when you know me so much better?"

Now I have written about both.

MOZAMBIQUE
MAKONDE
Figure 11 • Mphingo and White Hardwood

Most of the Makonde people live in Mozambique, although they extend across the border into southern Tanzania. I even discovered a cooperative of Makonde carvers in Arusha, in northeastern Tanzania.

Highly stylized and macabre masks comprise the Makondes' principal carvings. Some of their fame rests on their ability to use *mphingo*, an extremely hard wood that is black at the center and does not crack easily. When the Makonde carvers in numerous small villages in southeastern Tanzania execute their intricate sculptures, which can take as long as six to twelve months to complete, many small scraps are discarded. These two- to six-inch pieces are used to create chess sets.

There are about thirty million mphingo trees in Tanzania and in parts of southern Kenya, but the supply of mature trees is steadily decreasing. In the past, mphingo trees survived the natural grass fires that swept across the plains; their branches were barely singed. Now, because of the expansion of the rural population, more and more fires are deliberately set to clear land for farming. These more frequent hot fires tend to destroy the tender mphingo seedlings. The Tanzanian government controls and allocates the scarce wood, and carvers are not allowed to cut down trees for materials.

A little-known fact is that mphingo is used in the manufacture of clarinets. Tanzania realizes over $1.5 million in exports yearly from this use alone.

The next time you listen to a clarinet, whether in a Benny Goodman jazz number or a classical piece, you may be hearing the rich tones produced by mphingo.

An unfortunate discovery by clarinet manufacturers is that, probably as a consequence of the deliberately set hot fires, recently cut mphingo wood has a tendency to develop hairline cracks, which ruin the completed instruments. Preliminary steps are underway to impose a modest concert or recording tax to create a fund for mphingo tree nurseries.

Maybe chess collectors will get involved in the funding effort, although I suspect that more people listen to the clarinet than play with Makonde chess sets made from mphingo.

Makonde • Pawn

MOZAMBIQUE
Figure 12 • Yellowwood and Ebony

This older example probably dates from the time Makonde sets began to proliferate, in about 1950, and before the influence of larger figures and cruder work approximating "airport art."

Although the style is similar to the previous much larger set described, the details are finer. The genitals of the full-length, unclothed males are carefully concealed by their hands. Faces reveal the common practice of scarification. The Pawns are all women holding cloth to cover their breasts. Castles are huts with doors similar to those of the previous set; but here the huts are depicted with grass-covered pitched roofs.

Bishop

THE COMOROS, COCOS, AND RODRIGUEZ

Ones that Got Away

Happily, the adventures of the search can more than compensate for grand hopes not realized. So it was when I failed to acquire ethnic chess sets from these sub-Saharan islands.

THE COMOROS

In the Indian Ocean between the northern tip of Madagascar and the southeast coast of Africa lie the Comoro Islands. On a visit in the 1980s, I stayed in a neat little hotel in Moroni on Grande Comoro, but I wanted to see the outer islands. The airline that made trolley stops on the islands had only one plane—a Fokker—and I was unable to get clear reservations. I could have been stuck for weeks. Luckily, at the hotel, I struck up a friendship with the pilot, an officer on leave from the Moroccan air force. We played chess on an outdoor board, with four-foot-high pieces. Our match was intense, and he won the deciding game. Afterwards I pressed my desire to visit all the islands. Being a gracious winner, he said that if I had a ticket he would let me fly in the radio operator's seat.

Our first stop was Anjouan, where Blackbeard the Pirate, otherwise known as Edward Teach, used to careen his ships to scrape off the barnacles that proliferated in the tropical seas. From there it was on to Moheli. These tropical islands have changed relatively little since the days when they were named the Spice Islands by Sinbad the Sailor. At our next stop, Mayotte, I was abruptly brought back to the modern world by the sight of a French nuclear submarine anchored in the harbor. Mayotte remains a French territory; it has a small French population and an air link with Reunion, a political department of metropolitan France.

The other Comoro islands (not including Mayotte), perpetually in debt, are members of the United Nations. For a while they were run by a modern French pirate who sailed two fishing boats in great secrecy all the way from southern France to Grande Comoro, where his one-hundred-plus freebooters captured the island of a half million people and ruled for a decade. Pirate rule was maintained with unofficial help from the South Africans. They found the Comoros a useful base from which to harass the Frelimo (Liberation Front) government in nearby Mozambique. I overheard a South African spy, ostensibly in Comoro on a snorkeling vacation, speaking quietly in Afrikaans about his underwater exploration of the reefs to find the best locations for landings.

Grande Comoro was useful in other ways too. Unmarked cargo planes carried South Africa's best-in-the-world G5 cannons there to be picked up by the Iraqis or their Kuwati friends. Eventually the Iranians outbid the Iraquis and took over the pickups.

The chess set I had in mind would have the British East Indians versus the pirates, with skull-and-crossbones markings. Blackbeard would make a grand King. The Knight would be a coelacanth, a fish that presumably had died out in the Cretaceous Period, more than sixty-five million years ago, although one was found by a South African zoologist in 1938. I had a chance to feel the stubby "arm" of a frozen coelacanth and, from that experience, could surmise that its cousin was the first fish to walk on land. Coelacanths are rare, live at great depths, and die when brought to the surface. They are so oily as to be inedible. But famous they are. I have a five-franc coin, issued by the Comoro treasury, with an engraving of a coelacanth on it. The fish would be a worthy Knight indeed.

Unfortunately, with all the political activity and spying to look into on the Comoro Islands, there wasn't time to arrange for a chess set. At least I wasn't picked up by the French mercenaries, tied to a lead weight, and dropped into the sea as shark bait—a fate experienced by some inquiring Europeans.

RODRIGUEZ

Rodriguez is a remote, barren, typhoon-lashed island in the Indian Ocean about six hundred miles east of Mauritius. Rodriguez was settled by the jetsam of pirate ships and Portuguese and French shipwrecks. Some African slaves were also deposited on the island, which had not been inhabited by humans before the early 1500s.

Different species of the now extinct dodo bird once inhabited both Mauritius and Rodriguez. The flightless birds were about the size of a large turkey and apparently had no natural enemies for thousands of years. Then man arrived on the islands. The Mauritius dodo disappeared by the late 1600s. The Rodriguez dodo, which laid a single egg in a nest made of palm leaves, was faster and more difficult to capture than the Mauritius species; each wingtip had a heavy knob that was used as a weapon. It managed to survive until about 1800. The birds are known now only by their skeletal remains.

The chess set I designed with a local carver—but never got—was to have the Rodriguez dodo as Knight, a pirate as King, and a sailing ship as Castle.

COCOS

It is a geographical stretch to include Cocos in a book on sub-Saharan Africa, but I'm taking that liberty because my visits to the island are always associated with Africa.

In the 1950s Qantas's longest-range plane was the Lockheed Constellation. The route from Perth, Australia to Johannesburg, South Africa required stops at Cocos and Mauritius. The first time I flew it, the plane could carry barely half a load because of the heavy fuel needs.

The Cocos Archipelago, in the Indian Ocean northwest of Australia, is now a territory of that country. At the time of my visits in the 1950s, though, the islands were privately owned by the Clunies-Ross family. The plantation on Home Island had produced copra for five generations, beginning with John Clunies-Ross in 1825, and using local Malays for labor. Recently the copra business has fallen off and the ancestral home—painted a brilliant white, with beautifully timbered rooms and a walled garden—was up for sale as a hotel in early 1991.

On my first stopover in Cocos I was intrigued by a local carver, an old Malay, who had laid out his scrimshaw on a canvas strip near the airport lounge. (Then, as now, there were no tourist or antique shops in Cocos.) He had produced extraordinary carvings on a multitude of local seashells. We discussed the possibility of his making a chess set, and I left him a small token of my interest. Although we exchanged addresses, he never used mine.

A few years later, in the Qantas departure lounge in Perth awaiting another flight to Africa, I explained about the hoped-for Cocos seashell chess set to a charming woman who, as it turned out, was the daughter of the Australian High Commissioner in Cape Town. She invited me to join her in first class and, although we arrived in Cocos in the middle of the night, she arranged for a car to take us to the carver's home. I anticipated disappointment, and I was right. The carver was out fishing; his wife knew nothing about the set.

Because we still had three hours before the plane left for Mauritius, I welcomed her suggestion that we go to the beach. The sand sparkled dazzling white in the moonlight, and the fluorescent waves shone like a million fireflies. Both sand and water were invitingly warm. We separated in the shadows to remove our clothing and went for a long swim along the shoreline.

When we returned to the airport the Qantas manager noticed my companion's wet hair and expressed great concern that an accident had befallen this diplomatic personage.

"Oh," she said, with a toss of her head, "Ned and I had the most wonderful swim."

The manager's face turned a bilious yellow. "You shouldn't have! There's been a terrible infestation of Portuguese men-of-war. One man has died, and four are in the infirmary."

Ships call rarely at Cocos now. If you should sail the four thousand miles of open ocean from Mauritius to Perth, do stop for a break at Cocos, but check before you go in the water. And keep an eye open. Maybe my chess set is ready. ▦

PART TWO

WESTERN AFRICA

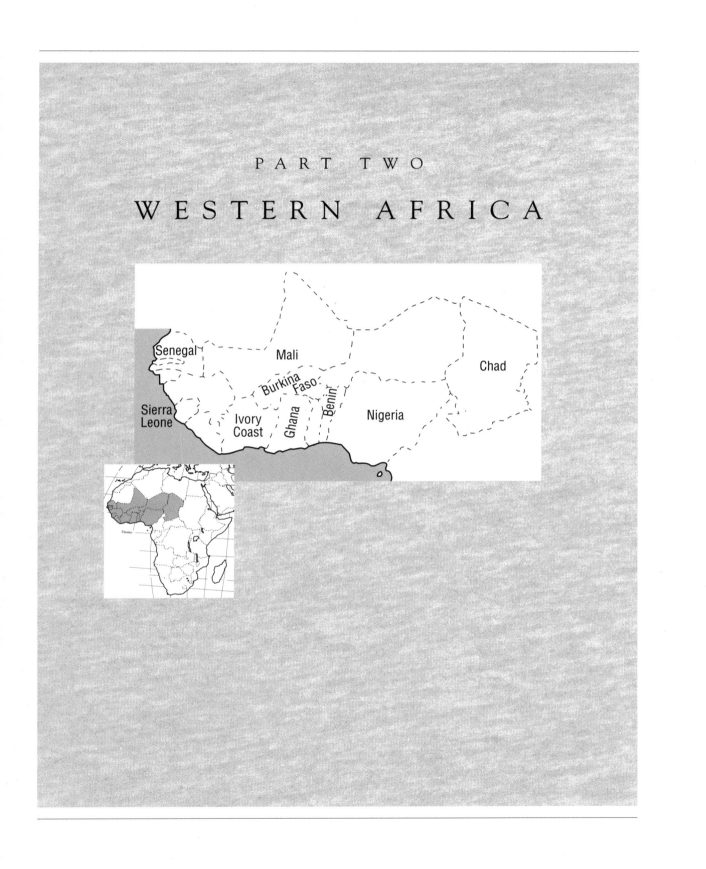

BENIN

Figure 13 • Glazed Ceramic

Some years ago I stood in the central square of Benin's largest city, Cotonou, and felt at an ideological crossroads. On one side of the square was an enormous Roman Catholic cathedral. Across from it was the headquarters of the Marxist-dominated ruling party; a huge red banner extolling the virtues of Leninism was draped across its façade. On a third side were stalls selling all manner of exotic traditional medicines, which have been available in Benin for centuries, and in whose efficacy a majority of the people believe. One "business" consisted of only a chair on which was propped a painted board with illustrations of four hairdos and a blunt statement that read: "No credit to anyone over 90 unless accompanied by a grandmother." (I bought the sign.) The fourth side of the square was lined with large stores selling European-made goods, representing the newer religion of capitalism.

Merchants in both the formal and informal sectors were able to make large profits from smuggling goods into Nigeria, just east of Benin. A planeload of flashlight batteries, one hundred cases of Johnny Walker or Chanel No. 5, to cite actual examples, could be sold for twice their landed cost across the highly permeable border. Transactions were in dollars and were quite open.

Benin was called Dahomey while it was under French colonial rule. Even before that, the traditional seat of power was in the town of Abomey where a long reign of kings were celebrated in oral tradition and art.

Famous for its legendary Amazon women warriors, Benin has another claim to fame, of sorts. The country was used as a stand-in for Haiti in the filming of a Graham Greene mystery, *The Comedians*. Elizabeth Taylor also made a film there. Former Caltech student Pat Manning, who took one of my courses and, against my advice, abandoned a career in chemistry for one in African Studies, ran into the famous star while in Benin (then Dahomey) for his doctoral dissertation research.

Bishop

This striking set—one side black and red, the other terra cotta and blue—was made by Margaret Robinson, the multi-talented African American artist from Los Angeles who, as you read earlier, did not object to bowing to Kabaka Mutebi when she presented him with another chess set. She came from an accomplished family with its roots in Arkansas, graduated from San Francisco State University, and began her professional career as a reporter for the *Chicago Defender*, *Jet*, and *Ebony*.

Three burglaries in her Crenshaw neighborhood storefront studio resulted in long delays in completing the set. She had to close down and temporarily lost the use of her large kiln. Whites tend to forget that most victims of so-called black crime are African Americans, even in solidly middle class areas such as the Crenshaw district of Los Angeles.

The chess set is unusual in that the Bishop, a totem representing ancestral spirits and religious figures, is taller than the King. While there is a resemblance in the beaded collars of the King and Queen to their cousins in the Yoruba of Western Nigeria, the actual representation is pure Dahomeyan. The Knight is a leopard, often featured in Dahomeyan legend. The Castle is part of the gate to the old palace in Abomey. Climbing over the gate tower is a serpent, a sign of wisdom in southern Dahomey.

MAUNOURY'S FAUX CHESS SET

Figure 14

Knight

That passion can lead to moral blindness and impaired judgment is well known. Jean Maunoury, the greatest French chess collector of all time, was not immune to the unruly passion of collecting. After considering the evidence, you may agree with me that this so-called nineteenth-century, teak chess set from West Africa is an example of passion unbridled if not unscholarly.

In *Collecting: An Unruly Passion*,[1] Werner Muensterberger, a practicing psychoanalyst, presents a well-researched historical examination of what has motivated collectors through the ages. However, to me, the book is a far less satisfactory examination of collecting from a psychological perspective. Muensterberger emphasizes that collecting is a reaction to a deprived childhood; he theorizes that the motivation to collect stems from childhood anal retention, among other things. The author interviewed a number of famous collectors. He offers examples of the passion that drives some collectors to pay the price of family, honor, wealth, and even life itself. He limns the tensions of the auction effectively.

In his book review Adam Phillips praises the author for his "assiduous collecting of collectors" but concludes that the book is overly reductive and "like too many psychoanalytic books is for people who like believing we are all the same, that there is only one story and we already know what it is."[2]

Collectors are aware that many dealers, and even fellow collectors, make it a habit to gild the lily when describing their chess sets. David Hafler of Philadelphia, who is probably the leading collector in the United States at this time, commented to me that Alex Hammond never sold a chess set without including a tale that enhanced its value. Hafler said, "The longer I collect, the more I have to try to avoid cynicism; but I have become less trusting."

―――――

Despite its distinguished provenance, this incomplete set of seven chess pieces poses a puzzle that may be related to the vagaries of collectors.

Maunoury had a fabulous collection of ancient and modern sets of great beauty. This incomplete set from his Cannes collection is illustrated and described by Hans and Siegfried Wichmann in their classic book.[3] An entire page is devoted to a picture of the King and Queen. The Wichmanns, who are known for their integrity and attention to detail, label the set as nineteenth-century West African, attribute its provenance only to Maunoury, and describe the material as teak.

Hafler acquired the pieces as part of a larger purchase from the Maunoury collection. They were illustrated in the catalog of the Chess Sets Auction held in New York by South Bay Auctioneers on May 28, 1990, in conjunction with a meeting of Chess Collectors International. It was there that I bought them.

―――――

Without a history, I would not know how to date these seven pieces. Chess sets from sub-Saharan Africa are rarely very old. The oldest one I know of is the Welled Selasse set discussed in the introduction to this volume.

So the question remains: Does this incomplete Maunoury set actually date from the nineteenth century?

The material of the set is also questionable. According to the Wichmanns, it is teak. Although the teak tree (Tectona grandis) is now cultivated in West

Africa, it is not native to that region but to India, Indonesia, and Malaysia. Perhaps the pieces are made from another dark wood, such as ebony. Most African ebony is brownish in color, but ebony chess sets from Africa have often been made black by the vigorous application of shoe polish.

The Wichmanns' descriptions of the pieces also raise questions. For example, they say the Pawn is an orangutan. I have some knowledge of orangutans because, as president of the Leakey Foundation, I participated in grants to Jane Goodall for the study of chimpanzees in Tanzania; the late Dian Fossey for the study of gorillas in Rwanda; and Birute Galdikas for the study of orangutans in Borneo. In the nineteenth century, when this chess set was supposedly created, the European press—particularly in England—stirred up a lot of racist nonsense relating Africans to higher apes. There was much confusion about the great apes, but no one ever saw an orange-looking orangutan in West Africa.

There is also a problem relating the chess pieces to a particular part of West Africa. Cameroon comes closest. The Wichmanns describe the King as having mutton chop whiskers. Such hirsute adornment is rare in West Africa, although the rulers in Dahomey and Yorubaland did partially cover their faces. Also, I do not recognize the crown described by the Wichmanns. I have raised the question with the surviving Wichmann, through Thomas Thomsen, without reply.

When I relayed my skepticism to David Hafler, he was not surprised. (Remember that he had acquired the pieces incidentally, as part of a larger purchase, without any particular regard for them.) He reported that, when the pieces were still part of his collection, they were seen by an expert on African art who was as doubting as I am of their nineteenth-century West African origin. The expert pointed out that the white pigment found in the eyes of the springer (Knight) is not consistent with that claimed origin.

Why were the Wichmanns not more critical of the pieces, I wondered, inasmuch as they provided such technical details and so much space to them in their book? Hafler thinks they simply accepted what Maunoury had also apparently accepted when he bought them.

Of course I was guilty of the same blind acceptance. I believed that such attention to detail by the well-reputed authors of a superb book meant that the pieces were as claimed: nineteenth-century West African teak. At least I won't sell them as other than a fascinating fake footnote to chess set history.

SENEGAL

Figure 15 • Cast Brass

This set was bought at Phillips in London. One side was described as "dark patinated." Although cast, examples of the same chess pieces vary considerably.

When I asked the curator why the set was called "Senegalese," he said, "Because that is how Victor Keats describes it in his book."[4]

The next day, while visiting Keats at his home in the Downs to see his handsome chess collection, I asked him the origin of the name. "Because I bought it in Dakar," he said.

Fair enough. If the famous Charlemagne pieces in the Bibliotheque National—which may be contemporary with the German emperor, but almost certainly were never seen by him—can be called "Charlemagne," then this set can be called "Senegalese," although many features of the set make me think of it as generic West African.

Bishop

The Knights are clearly modeled after the well-known Bambara style of African antelope. Mali is the ancestral home of the Bambara. The Kings and Queens are seated on stools that are associated with the Akan peoples—the Baoule in the Ivory Coast and the Fante in Ghana. The stool denotes the throne of a ruler. Indeed, the Golden Stool of the Asanthehene (King) in Kumasi is famous in anthropology. The Asanthehene's umbrella shielding him from the sun is characteristic. The Queens have the prominent navel so often seen in West Africa.

The Bishops are spiritual figures in differing styles, one side wearing an antelope headdress and a tail, the other holding objects aloft. The huts used as Castles do have a baobab look about them, and you see many such trees in the semi-desert of Senegal.

The pawns vary widely. Some carry a pot on their heads, others are eating, and still others have hands in different positions. I suspect that the pieces are interchangeable, depending on the makeup of an individual set.

SIERRA LEONE
CREOLES VS. MENDE
Figure 16 and Cover • Wood

Creole • King

Sierra Leone was a proud country when I first visited there in 1948. For a century it had the only university in British West Africa. Many of the leaders—government officials, judges, teachers—in The Gambia, in Ghana, and particularly in Nigeria were from the crown colony of Sierra Leone.

In the mid-twentieth century, the country was divided into two parts: the colony, which surrounded the capital of Freetown and was populated largely by Creoles; and the territory, which was the home of the indigenous peoples. To the extent that there was self-government in the colony, the franchise was exercised by the Creoles. They considered themselves elite. At best they tolerated the populace of the territory; at worst they looked upon it with contempt.

The Creoles themselves came from divers sources. In 1787 a settlement was started for the blacks who had fought for the British in the American Revolution and for runaway slaves who had made their way to London. The settlement failed in part because of hostility among the indigenous people represented. In 1791 the survivors were collected into Granville, a new settlement promoted by Granville Sharp and William Wilberforce, both British abolitionists. The following year John Clarkson, a lieutenant in the British Navy, brought 1,100 Africans from Nova Scotia to the settlement, which was moved back to its original site and named Freetown. Zachary Macaulay, father of the well-known British historian, was governor at the time, and helped the settlement survive a plundering by the French. The slaves carried as cargo in ships captured by the Royal Navy were also released in Freetown rather than being returned to their African masters on the West African Coast.

As I write this, I have before me an original letter written with quill pen on September 3, 1793 by Thomas Clarkson, the abolitionist and brother of John Clarkson, acknowledging receipt of £50 for a share of the Sierra Leone Company. Things must have been looking up for the freed slaves in Freetown because Clarkson wrote, "It is with peculiar pleasure I assure you that our news from S. Leone is of the most flattering nature."

Years ago in the country of Jamaica I visited Akropong, one of the many isolated villages established by runaway slaves from all over West Africa in the seventeenth century. (Akropong is also the name of a village in Ghana.) Those who settled in the interior of Jamaica were known as Maroons. The name probably has nothing to do with being shipwrecked. More likely it comes from the Spanish *cimarron*, meaning wild or untamed. The Maroons, encouraged by the Spanish, were a sharp thorn in the British side for more than 160 years. The small British forces never succeeded in defeating them. Finally a treaty was worked out; the Maroons were moved to Nova Scotia. However, they found the climate inhospitable and, after a few generations, were brought to Freetown by John Clarkson, as noted above. There was a "Maroontown" in the capital when I first visited. The Maroons have since merged with the Creoles.

In the past, the Creoles lorded it over the indigenous "bush" peoples of the interior who were legally protected persons outside the Sierra Leone Colony. In this the Creoles were like the American-Liberians in Liberia who, in 1948 when I wrote a thesis on that country, dominated and despised the "natives." In Sierra Leone it was long after World War II that anything approaching legal equality developed between the Creoles and the indigenous peoples who so dominate the country's politics. Now, to a large extent, the Creoles have merged with the more numerous indigenous peoples.

The Mende are one of the more fascinating ethnic groups in Africa. Their complex masks, an expression of their traditional religion, are famous in the western art world. Mende society is complicated. The one million people are divided into those who are initiated into a secret society (*hale*) and those who are not (*kpowa*). Many traditional Mende practices, including the secret societies, female circumcision, and polygyny

(with each wife having her own hut) have become less common with modernization and western education. In 1975 I published a study of Sierra Leone politics written by Filomina Chioma Steady, who was originally from Freetown.[5] Chioma is a Timmoney name that stresses the power of women in decision making among the Mende and in the country in general.

The Mende are also distinct among ethnic groups in West Africa in that, in pre-European times, they developed their own ideographic writing system in which each character represents a syllable. Some erudite Mende families have been fluent in Arabic and English for perhaps eight generations. Still, very little ideographic writing has been translated because the Mende do not believe the thousand nuances of their secret society should be known to outsiders.

The chess set was commissioned for me by Amy Bongay, a Mende from Sierra Leone who operated an African crafts shop in Pasadena. The artist-carver, Tsiaka O. Lawal, lives in Freetown and comes from a local Fourah Bay tribe.

The reddish pieces in this chess set portray the Creoles. The Pawns are unusual in two ways: they are female, a rarity in ethnic sets; and, because they wear the tall headdress of Creole women, they are larger than the King and Queen. The other side, representing the Mende, also has a feature unusual in African sets: a baboon is used for the Knight.

IVORY COAST
BAOULE
Figure 17 • Resin and Wire

The Afrikaans expression *heeltemal deurmekaar* (completely mixed up) aptly describes the ethnic identity of this set bought in South Africa. It was sold to me in

Bishop

1992 as "Venda," one of the so-called Bantu home-lands in the Transvaal before independence. But I could find no Venda-speaking person who could catch a glimmer of Venda culture in the pieces. The Vendas have a fascinating history, which is unfolding with new scholarship. It relates their movement south from present-day Zimbabwe over the last few hundred years. However, "Venda" is a false trail in regard to the origin of this set, which was made in the Transvaal.

You can see why the ethnic identity of the set is in question. The base friezes on all the pieces bear an African motif. But the King has an Asian cast to his countenance and wears an Asian-styled loincloth. The Queen also looks Asian. And there is an Asian look to the Bishop, with his long face, beard, and cap over his ears. (This may be the only chess set in which the Bishop displays his penis.) The Knight rides a water buffalo, native to southern Asia, Malaysia and the Philippines.

On the other hand, the drum-shaped Castle is distinctly Akan, a people prominent in both Ghana and the Ivory Coast, where they are known as Baoule. The Baoule, and their cousins the Ashanti, are renowned for their carved stools—a symbol of chieftainship. The Pawns display African lips and hairdos, but there is nothing African in their submissive posture or the cleft of their exposed buttocks.

Flaws are not uncommon in ethnic sets—a mix of customs from different historical periods, characteristics borrowed from neighboring ethnic groups, features from bordering countries. However, this set suggests a deliberate combination of two widely diverse cultures, Baoule and Asian.

The erroneous appellation "Venda" illustrates how some manufacturers will attach any name to a product if they think it will sell. The molds for this set, which is made of resin with interior metal supports, are included in a catalog of a dozen chess set molds, all designed for use with various materials and produced in Hull, England at modest prices.

Burkina Faso • King

BURKINA FASO
Figure 18 • Iron

When I acquired this set in 1952, in the capital city of Ouagadougou, Burkina Faso was called Upper Volta and had not yet won independence from the French.

It was a country without a railroad, although the French had built a handsome station in expectation that the line from Abidjan in the Ivory Coast would soon arrive. When I was there again in 1962, the station was being repaired from the ravages of torrential downpours and the harmattan (a hot, dry wind out of the Sahara that causes the humidity to drop sharply and, therefore, makes the body feel cooler). But the railroad had not yet arrived. It has now.

Handmade near the Mali border on the southern edge of the Sahara, the chess sets were carried by ubiquitous Hausa traders and were found throughout West Africa. But the last time I was in "Wag"—as the capital is dubbed in local slang—in 1978, I could find none.

Why the Knights are so much taller than the Kings and Castles I have not yet been able to find out. The bright colors tend to be similar in all the sets and are also used on individual metal figures sold to the passing trade.

MALI
Figure 19 and Cover • Gold and Black Metal

In 1994 the colorfully painted iron Burkina Faso sets, which have been virtually unchanged for at least fifty years, stimulated a Mali version created by what I believe was a breakaway group of craftsmen. Although this new set style is a crude knockoff, it does have distinct features.

A tower replaces the hut as Castle. An antelope, quite like the famous wooden figures with long graceful horns carved by the Bambara (a tribe in Mali), replaces the rearing horseman with his spear as Knight. Traditionally the Burkina Faso Knight was almost twice as tall as the Castle; in this Mali set the Knight is shorter than the Castle.

The tall Mali Kings and Queens have a sort of spiraled horn that rises one and one-half inches from their foreheads. The King holds his arms ramrod straight; the Queen cups her bosom. The Bishops are birdlike creatures. Although the Pawns are all from the same mold, the imperfections of casting tend to give their faces individual expressions.

A knowledgeable friend suggested that the Mali version seems to reflect a less animistic and perhaps more Islamic influence than the Burkina Faso style. That idea has merit; I'll be better able to comment on it when I've visited the place where the pieces are actually hammered out.

GHANA
ASHANTI

Figure 20 • Gold Weights

For centuries the Ashanti people have mined and sold gold. If you assay the original gold guineas of seventeenth-century England, you can ascertain the precise Ghanaian mine they came from by the distinctive combinations of metals associated with the gold, which was not pure.

The Ashantis traditionally weighed gold dust on a scale, with the dust on one side and gold weights of

known value on the other. Many books in German, English, and other languages describe and picture gold weights. Original gold weights from earlier centuries now sell for large sums at Sotheby's.

A New York artist known as Rima had the imagination to have molds made of some of the finest Ashanti weights and assembled a chess set from them.

The Pawns represent the bird *santrofio*, which symbolizes the expression *sankofa* (to go back). In the Akan culture, encompassing both Ashanti and Fanti, and extending to the Baoule people of the Ivory Coast, a mother would invoke the spirit of *santrofio* for sons or daughters going abroad, reminding them to return to their roots.

The Queen has the characteristic headgear (*abotre*) of a Fanti queen. The King is dressed with fetish amulets around his neck and on his arm, given to him by his chief to ward off evil spirits. His sword (*afra*) is typical.

The Bishop is symbolized by *akuaba*, a goddess representing the queen mother. This symbol is worn by barren women. The Knight is interesting because of the small size of the horse, and because the Ashanti did not normally have horses. The Castle is a typical man of the nineteenth century, with a double-rolled cloth around his waist.

In recent centuries, traditional Ghanaian religions were protected from the encroachment of Islam by the death-inflicting tsetse fly, which stopped the Islamic cavalry coming down from the Sahara. From the south the Ashanti were long protected from conquest (and in fact were never truly defeated) by the mosquito, which gave the Christian Europeans severe malaria. Thus, the Ashanti king flourished and sat on his Golden Stool for centuries, protected by insects and able to weigh gold dust with these gold weights.

Mali • King

Ghana • Pawn

NIGERIA
YORUBA VS. HAUSA
Figures 21a and 21b • Thornwood

The Nigerians had sophisticated art long before the Europeans invaded their shores. Bronze castings of the heads of Oba (king) from the fifteenth century can fetch almost a million dollars at auction.

Thorn carvings in Nigeria date from the 1930s. They are from the wood of the ata and egua egua trees, the finest of which grow in the Shagamu region. The colors are cream, rose, and brown. Most of the exquisite thorn carvings depict amusing scenes from Nigerian life. Those reaching Europe are made from different, contrasting pieces of wood glued together with a viscous paste made from rice.

One steamy day in January 1948 I was walking in Tinubu Square in Lagos, Nigeria, taking care not to fall into the open three-feet deep by two-feet wide sewers that were flushed out most days by a tropical storm. I came upon a young man sitting on the sidewalk carving thornwood pieces.

Thornwood can be carved in intricate detail, and he was doing moderately well with his raw talent. We chatted on that day and others during my visit. He told me that his name was Akeredolu and that he had dropped out of school. I taught him how to play chess, sitting on a corner of the busy square. Then, together, we designed a chess set which he agreed to carve for me. He was happy when I drew on my meager resources as a graduate student to pay him one dollar for each of the thirty-two pieces.

The set Akeredolu carved for me in 1948 represents two of the three largest ethnic groups of Nigeria, the Yoruba of the southwest and the Hausa of the north. Each piece is made from a single piece of wood.

The cream-colored wood was dyed black for contrast.

On the Yoruba side, the King is an Oba, the Queen a typical woman of royalty. The Bishop is a sorcerer, the Castle a grass hut. The Pawns are school children studying industriously.

The horse as the Yoruba Knight is an anomaly because horses are not common in southwestern Nigeria. As Azikwe, the president of Nigeria, remarked in 1953 when we talked to a group of students, insects were the greatest friends of the Nigerian people. The anopheles mosquito, the cause of malaria, was credited with keeping out the white settlers, just as it did in Ghana. The tsetse fly was reputed for keeping out the powerful cavalry of the Muslim invaders who came from the north. Horses south of the tsetse line die. But Akeredolu and I lacked the imagination to come up with another animal for the Knight.

On the Hausa side the King is an emir wrapped in his garments. The Queen is veiled. The Castle is a large mud structure from the dry north of Nigeria. Such an edifice would wash away in the torrential rains of the south. The Bishop is an Islamic Imam. The Knight is patterned after the magnificently caparisoned horses used from the sixteenth century to about 1900 by the Fulani (northern Muslims) to control the north. The Pawns are studying the Koran.

After my 1948 visit to Nigeria, I stayed in touch with Akeredolu, and made various suggestions to friends about his possible further education. Akeredolu did finish high school, took a diploma from the Slade School of Art in London, and returned to Nigeria to teach art in the Yaba Technical College, from which he retired a few years ago.

In April 1959, eleven years after I taught the sculptor to play chess and commissioned his first set, *Chess Review* featured an illustrated article describing

Yoruba • King

J. D. Akeredolu's chess pieces that were exhibited in western Nigeria's Illorin Museum.

Akeredolu may have stopped making chess sets in about 1960. Victor Keats writes: "Prior to 1960, it was possible, on very rare occasions, to obtain a wooden chess set of superlative quality and exquisite beauty made throughout by a wonderful carver named Akadula [sic] who worked in Lagos, Nigeria. He used selected thornwood and ebony when carving a chess set, and every piece was finished to utmost perfection in every respect. After Akadula [sic], a host of skilled craftsmen produced fine chess sets, but in spite of the very high quality seen in these most excellent products, the master craftsman's work stands alone."[6]

Did Akeredolu change the spelling of his name? Or is the spelling in Keats's book a phonetic error? I don't know, but I have used the name the sculptor carved on the base of his first set, the one he made for me that is pictured in figures 21a and 21b.

NIGERIA
SOUTH
Figure 22 • Thornwood

Akeredolu's success drew many imitators. One of them carved this set from light and dark thornwood glued together to form each piece.

Both sides represent the south and, particularly, the Yoruba from southwestern Nigeria. The Castles are thatched huts, common in the south. As in Akeredolu's set, the horse with rider as Knight is an anomaly.

It would be inaccurate to dichotomize Nigeria into a Muslim north and a Christian-Pagan south; about fifty percent of the Yoruba are Muslims. In this set the Bishops are clearly Christian.

One charming aspect of the Pawns, crude as they are, is that each has unique characteristics. They vary in size from 1¼ inches to 2¼ inches. Unfortunately, their swollen bellies make them look like children suffering from malnutrition.

AFRICAN-EUROPEAN
GRASS SKIRTS
Figures 23a and 23b • Porcelain

Bishop

Descriptions of this porcellaneous set are pusillanimous. Its origin seems to be mysteriously dubious, ascribed to various European countries. The white side is usually dubbed simply as European; the black side, described generically as African. It is not that there are no sources or ideas as to the pedigree of the set; *au contraire* there are too many. Consider:

Christies sale, April 3, 1980, Lot 108. Estimated: £300 - £400. Price: £130 plus 10%. "A Belgian porcelain set depicting African Negroes. The scantily dressed kings with beads, the queens bedecked with jewelry."

Sotheby's New York sale, June 8, 1993, item 22 illustrated #22. Estimated: $1,500 - $2,000. Price: $1,000. "German Porcelain Chess Set, Mid-Late 19th Century. The Europeans vs. the Africans, the kings and queens are crowned, the European king in multicolor dress, the bishops as marching figures and African busts, the knights as white vs. brown rearing horses, rook as towers, the pawns as busts. The Europeans in grey helmets, the Africans in tribal jewelry. Some minor chips."

Nigeria • King

Bonhams sale, May 17, 1994, Number 98 not illustrated but referenced to Keats. Estimated: £600 - £700. Price: unsold. "An Austrian porcelain figural Chess Set, painted black and white. Africa opposing Europe, the kings and queens as monarchs, the bishops (laufers) as a running child, the knights as rearing horses, the rooks as a tower, the pawns as busts of soldiers in armour, and a child. See Keats for similar but coloured example."

Keats, Victor. CHESSMEN FOR COLLECTORS. London: Batsford, 1985, p.60 Ill. 61. "Austrian porcelain fairy tale chessmen, designed as fanciful native black Africans, twentieth century."

USA Collection of Ernst and Sonya Boehlen. "5393 Germany, polychrome porcelain, all marked with blue "H", 20th Cent., the amusing figures as Africans vs. Europeans, the native African king and queen wearing skirts and with crowns, the European monarchs in medieval attire, the bishops either as African or European "Laufer," the later in medieval attire, the knights as rearing horses, the rooks as towers, the pawns as half-length figures either African or as armored European warriors. (For African side, see Keats. According to Keats the set is from Austria.)"

So the question remains: where and when was this set made? I contacted several well-known collectors to try to get the answer.

Collector David Hafler first saw examples of this set in a Copenhagen shop in the 1960s. The shop's owner, now deceased, bought them from a distributor who came regularly from East Germany. Hafler was told that the sets began to be produced somewhere in eastern Germany in about 1960. If that's true, then Sotheby's "Mid-Late 19th Century" date is incorrect.

Hafler bought three of the sets at the amazingly low price of $30 each. He gave one to Victor Keats and sold another to a fellow Philadelphia collector, Sam Bronstein, at the same price. Bronstein's collection was eventually purchased by the eminent Swiss collector Ernst Boehlen. During a visit to Dr. Boehlen in his Florida condominium, where he keeps a number of sets including some duplicates from his humongous Swiss collection, I purchased my "European-African" set for $3,500.

The distinguishing mark on the bottom of all pieces is a blue H or #. Franz Josef Lang, an expert on markings, immediately determined that the set was from East Germany.

I asked Keats how he had decided on Austria as the set's country of origin. He replied that he had compared this set with another (No. 60) in his book, which he was sure was Austrian, and the two sets had similar markings. He added, "Upon reflection, I have no evidence that they are Austrian except that I was told so. If they are not Austrian they most certainly emanate from some other European country...thinking aloud...yes, I feel they must be Austrian."

When I asked Keats how he explained calling the black side African, he said, "In providing them with African origin I had reckoned without Ned Munger. They are *fanciful* figures and one would not suppose that the European artist was trying to produce anything more than a cartoon of the natives." Clearly the artist was not sensitive to how pejorative such native cartoons are to Africans.

From my long experience in every African country and island during the course of eighty-nine visits in the past forty years, I find it difficult to go along with the African attribution. I have never seen Africans in yellow grass skirts—or any grass skirts. I have seen many grass skirts in the south seas, but never in Africa. Furthermore, I have not seen African women with long, straight, black hair as shown on the black Queen. There is no indication of North African representation; nor is the black side accurate for West Africa because, as noted earlier, horses, used as Knights on the black side, do not survive the tsetse fly there. The Bishops and Castles are also hopelessly out of character on the so-called African side. It would not have been difficult for the maker of this set to create a simple mold of an African hut for the Castle.

Of course designers may do as they wish, but the road to historical accuracy is pocked with such pitfalls as cultural bias and its adjunct, stereotypes. The black side of the set in question reveals several examples. The Queen is bare breasted. Her pupils seem to be rolling upward in the whites of her eyes, a characteristic of nineteenth-century black American comics. The African Pawns appear to be young children, a poor match for the steel-helmeted European Pawns. Even the African Bishops seem more childlike than the young European runners.[7]

At any rate, the mystery surrounding the origin of the set was finally solved for me by Hans Joachim Tinti, an intrepid chess set explorer. Tinti said the set was designed by Max Siegel and first produced in 1952 by Alfred Voigt, who owns Sitzendorfer Porzellanfacktur, established in 1850 in what was East Germany. Sets are still being made for interested collectors.[8]

Perhaps three morals can be drawn from this tale. First, when chess set designers venture outside their own culture and time, they are apt to commit errors. Second, major auction houses are not perfect; they can arrive at strikingly different judgments about the same set, even though they employ genuine experts and rely on leading collectors for advice. And third, prices can vary wildly, as evidenced by the fact that I paid more than one hundred times as much for the set as David Hafler did. (Of course his purchase occurred about thirty years earlier than mine, when the factor of East German currency was different from what it is today.)

Although it is a bizarre set, I've learned much from owning an example of it.

CHAD
GENERICALLY ETHNIC
Figure 24 • Wood

Queen

Africa is often behind the times when it comes to modern equipment. The first time I flew into Chad, in 1951, it was in a Tin Goose, an all-metal Fokker single engine plane from 1928. Not many pilots flew it without becoming deaf.

We landed in Fort Lamy, as N'Djamena was then known. The ambience was right out of Beau Geste, complete with fort and Foreign Legionnaires. The French pilot apologized that there was no room available in his Air Chance guest house. He drove me to a two-story, crumbling, mud and brick building. The sign read "HO*EL."

It did have a vacant room. As it turned out, all the other guests were women who appeared to be plying their trade for the benefit of the French soldiers blanc 'n noire. Fortunately my bone tiredness saved me from any nocturnal sounds.

In the morning I got up early, brushed off the bedbugs, and surveyed Fort Lamy. That night again I was the only male in my accommodations, but this time the women were Catholic nuns.

Chad has long intrigued me as a crossroads between north and south, east and west. The country was wracked by civil wars in the 1970s and 1980s. One of my Caltech colleagues, a mathematics professor, had a son stationed in northern Chad as a Protestant missionary—a delicate position in that predominantly Muslim country. Using a pseudonym, he wrote an account of the civil wars.[9] Those wars, the coups, and even the 1983 war between Chad and Libya, which ended disastrously for the Libyans, have not been exclusively religious in nature. Tribal animosities and personality conflicts were also factors.

Traditionally, political dominance had been held by the northern, Muslim-Arabphone half of the country. Beginning with French colonialism of Chad in the nineteenth century, that tradition was reversed. The French and the subsequent Chadian administrations were drawn from the better-educated people of the south, those who received their education from the Christian missions. This was a dramatic change from the days when the Arabic-speaking northerners captured black Africans in the animist south and shipped them as slaves to the Middle East or to Nigerian ports for transatlantic passage.

Chad is splintered not only by ethnicity and religion but by language. Northerners speak either Arabic or Gorane, an African language. In the south at least two hundred languages are spoken. Only French, the official language of the country, lends linguistic unity.

While surveying the sources of African chess sets, I contacted my colleague's son in Chad, and he agreed to have a set made for me. It took a year to get the set, partly because of communication problems. Persistent political and ethnic tensions also led to problems in working out who would be represented in the pieces. Eventually there was a fax from N'Djamena that the artist, Allahdoum Weko, had finished the set.

Weko is from the Kim tribe of the Mayo-Kebbi province halfway between N'Djamena and the southern part of the country. He attends the Ecole des Beaux Arts in the capital. His first name, which means "given by God (Allah)," is a typical Chadian mixture of Arabic and local tongue, and reflects a widespread belief that children are gifts of God. *Doum* means "to give" in a number of Chadian languages.

Weko had never seen a chess set before, but quickly got the idea. My set was to have a strictly ethnic theme, but the result was far less ethnic than I expected. I imagine Weko decided a definitive drawing of ethnic lines was too great a political risk. The two sides, brown and black, are almost identical. As in most Muslim sets, the pieces are not heavily representational. However, the faces and hairdos of the Kings and Queens do show gender differences, as would be expected in pieces depicting the animist-Christian south. Why the artist chose to make all the major pieces the same height is a question to be answered. As I recall them, the northerners tend to be tall and lean; the southerners, shorter and rounder. ▣

PART THREE
CENTRAL AFRICA

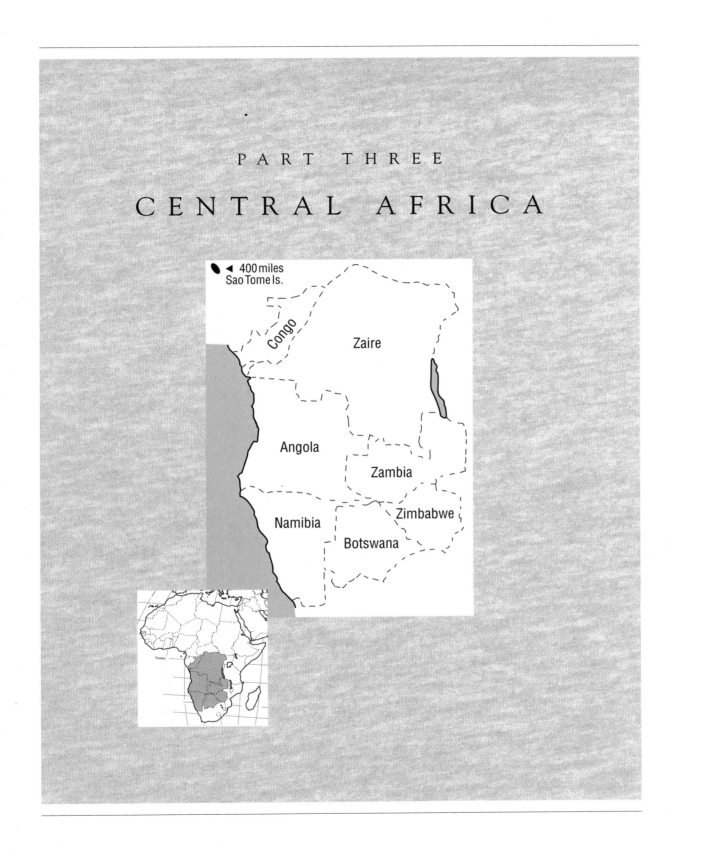

400 miles
Sao Tome Is.

Congo

Zaire

Angola

Zambia

Namibia

Zimbabwe

Botswana

Equator

ZAIRE

Figure 25 • Ivory

Fires burned throughout the city. Smoke rose from the waterfront. That is what Charles Collingwood of CBS, my old friend David Reed of *U.S. News and World Report*, and I saw as we stood on the north bank of the Congo River one day in 1960 and looked across at what was then Leopoldville (now Kinshasa). We were waiting for a ferry.

When it nosed into the wharf, about 250 terrified Belgians streamed off. Some expressed relief; some, anger. A priest swore at us Americans. He said in French, "I cannot understand why the Congolese are such savages. I've worked with them for forty years, slept with their women, and treated them as I would my own children. Now they turn on us."

One man approached us dangling car keys. Would we like to buy his new Mercedes parked on the opposite shore? He wanted $1,000 for it. When we didn't respond, he lowered the price to $100, "Americain." It would certainly have been a bargain. I might have accepted it if I thought there was a chance of finding the car in one piece, and if I thought I could have driven it the length of the Congo and into Tanzania or Zambia without being murdered by mutineers.

Leopoldville was a shambles—the scene of pillage, rape, and murder. Panicked by the fires, the Belgians had grabbed silver teapots, stuffed dolls, watches, anything, as they ran for their lives and boarded the ferry for Brazzaville. Here, on the dock, they were trying to sell their belongings. They needed cash for plane tickets, to complete their escape. Among the items for sale was a wooden cigar box. In it I found this ivory chess set. I didn't know what would happen to me in

subsequent days, but safely tucked in my knapsack was my latest purchase.

King

We three Americans were the only passengers to board the ferry. The crew was extremely nervous as we chugged toward the billowing smoke across the Stanley Pool, a four-mile stretch in the Congo River.

To call that water a pool makes it sound benign. But, as I found out a few days later, it's not. When the journalists wanted to file their stories, we found a motorboat on the dock at Leopoldville and started back to Brazzaville. Halfway across the pool, we ran out of gas. In the sudden quiet we could hear the menacing din of the great rapids a few miles down the river. As we drifted swiftly downstream, I took small comfort in knowing I had left the chess set in my Leopoldville hotel room. A small can of gas found hidden in the bottom of the boat saved us from calamity.

Great African art is by no means spread evenly across the sub-Sahara. It is virtually restricted to a narrow coastal bank along West Africa, and to southwestern Zaire. The prehistoric Zimbabwe stonework and the cave paintings of eastern, southern, and southeast Africa are also important. Great art does exist from the old Congo, but the only chess sets I have seen during many journeys there have been quite crude.

This set, acquired under circumstances more sanguinary than sanguine, is above average in detail. The bearded King carries a dagger; the Queen holds a whisk made of hair. The Knight wears a loincloth and aims a bow and arrow. The Bishop is a warrior with a raised spear; the Castle, a drummer; the Pawns, warriors with spears and shields.

Knight

Ivory • Bishop

CONGO

Figure 26 • Wood, Burlap, and Chicken Feathers

Herman Regusters, an African American, traveled far into northeastern Congo through areas probably never before seen by an outsider, intrepidly searching for a lost dinosaur. He thinks a small version of a dinosaur may have survived into the present—something like Bigfoot, the Loch Ness Monster, and other legendary characters. Locals in Congo call it *mokele-mbembe* and believe it eats humans.

For several horrendous weeks Regusters marched through snake-filled swamps, besieged by insects and accompanied by friendly chimps and gorillas. Although he did not positively see mokele-mbembe, he did return with fuzzy photographs of a supposedly mysterious animal and a tape recording of strange night sounds.

If he had not been a respected engineer and consultant for the Jet Propulsion Laboratory, I would have had trouble stifling a chuckle when he brought me his story. Although I remain thoroughly skeptical of the existence of a living dinosaur, I did publish Regusters's manuscript about it.[1]

Regusters now successfully imports *Ngok'* beer, named after the crocodile, from Brazzaville. He keeps returning to the Congo to search for his dinosaur. I hope he finds it. I can't prove that a ten-foot species hasn't survived, and that someone somewhere in the Congo hasn't already made a chess set with mokele-mbembe as the Knight.

The Congo River forms the southwestern boundary between Congo and Zaire. Brazzaville, Congo is on the north bank opposite Kinshasa, Zaire. This set was a gift from Regusters, who bought it in the large market in Brazzaville. It is almost identical to a set I

bought in Zaire in 1991. I suspect there are several sources of this style, which was first produced in about 1989. Once a product sells, it has many imitators. The materials cost next to nothing on both sides of the river.

CONGO

Figure 27 and Cover • Ebony and Ivory

Brazzaville, now the capital of the Congo, was also capital of the former French Congo and French Equatorial Africa. The city was the fulcrum of the De Gaulle Free French effort to push north and influence the fighting in Egypt's Western Desert during World War II. It was also involved in the logistical problems of sending American planes to the Middle East; short-range fighters, in particular, had to make numerous stops across Africa.

The American consul-general in Brazzaville in the 1940s was a young Berkeley-trained American Foreign Service officer named Lawrence Taylor, who had formed a strong bond with one of his house servants. Taylor found that the young man had artistic talent, so he encouraged a sort of cottage industry in his back shamba. Work was hard to find in those days, and state department wages, even for menial posts, were far above the local wage rate. I don't know how the servant was rewarded, but word of mouth has it that he carved this set as an act of admiration and thanks to his American employer.

In time Taylor moved back to the United States. He got to know my Caltech friends Virginia and Harold Wayland, themselves inveterate collectors of historical playing cards and other objects. They had admired Taylor's chess set on numerous occasions, and Taylor eventually gave it to them. Later the

Waylands allowed me to acquire it from them for a reasonable sum.

———————

Clearly, the artist relied on his own experience in designing the set. It is the only set I have even seen in which the Knight is depicted as the ubiquitous goat. Of course the selection of a goat instead of, say, a lion is not surprising for an African who based his work on personal experience. Most Africans have never seen a lion in the bush or even in a zoo. (I'll never forget the time I met a student protégé from Nigeria at the docks in New York. We had a day to spend sightseeing, so I asked what he preferred to do. He said, "Oh, can we go to the zoo and see lions? I was embarrassed on the ship when Europeans asked me about lions; I had never seen one in Africa.")

Many African sets have Castles that depict inexpensive huts, thrown together with palm leaves over wooden frameworks. In this set the Castle hut shows greater permanence and quality. It is made of carefully molded, sun-dried clay bricks neatly stacked to form the walls. The thatched roof is also neatly done, rising to a point that may be metal.

The Bishops are decorated with beads, as good sangomas should be, and appear to hold rattles. Why they are crowned escapes me. Clearly they are not Kings; they are a full inch shorter than the Kings.

Although the Pawns are undistinguished, their toes are carefully carved. It seems that the making of this set was a longtime labor of love.

The artist's personal experience is revealed again in the King and Queen. The Queen is modeled on the carver's wife, according to Taylor. Her hair is arranged in stylish cornrows; she is wrapped in a traditional blanket dress that is tucked into itself in front and supports her baby in back; possibly she is pregnant.

The King is modeled on the headman of the artist's Congo village circa 1940. The figure is dignified, to be sure, but that wasn't enough for the artist. To impart authority and grandeur, he has the King carry a bag slung over his left shoulder. Furthermore, it is obvious that the carver borrowed facial features from General Jacques Philippe Leclerc, commander of the Free French forces in World War II, for the King. There is the mustache that turns up at the corners and the goatee. The short beard is not unknown among Africans around Brazzaville, but they are rarely hirsute enough to produce such a mustache.

Can one have any doubt that General Leclerc would have been flattered to lend his curled mustache to boost the status of a village headman?

ANGOLA

Figure 28 • Perforated Ivory and Ebony

Mystery surrounds the ethnic origin of many African sets, forcing collectors to look for clues of attribution. Some sets reveal distinct ethnic markers: the geometric designs on Ndebele huts; the propensity of Xhosa women to smoke long pipes; the two-storied granaries of the Shangaan; the scarification of the Chokwe. Other sets appear to represent a blend of cultures.

Two major factors cause this problem of attribution. First, throughout African history, wars led to a thorough mixing of many populations. Second, there are many traveling artists who have their ethnic roots in one place, move to another part of the country, and eventually settle a thousand miles away, picking up artistic styles from various cultures and ethnic groups along the way.

Further problems arise in attempting to assign sets to particular countries. Students of Africa will know that it is arbitrary to call this set Angolan; it might just

Pawn

as accurately be assigned to Zimbabwe. Similarly, the Chokwe set assigned to Zimbabwe could be called Angolan. The homes of ethnic groups often do not conform to the "white man's borders."

--- ✦ ---

A skilled Angolan carver made this set for me. I found him in the area of Matadi on the Congo River in Zaire. That region became heavily Angolan after the workers deserted the coffee plantations of northern Angola during the Portuguese counteroffensive to the revolution that led to independence in 1975. Although there are traces of several Angolan ethnic groups in this set, it does not appear to belong clearly to any particular one. It also contains style elements suggestive of Malawi and even far-off Zimbabwe.

But, to me, the beauty of a chess set lies in its art, not its origin. In this most unusual set, the pawns' faces are carved with great fidelity from oblong blocks. Unlike most ivory sets, in which the surface is smooth, here it is perforated—particularly on the white side. The crowned King is seated, his right hand resting on a staff. The Bishop (sangoma) is also seated. He holds a stick in one hand and a magic object in the other; there are tassels on his lower legs.

If you know of a similar set, please contact me. I would like to learn more about it.

ZAMBIA
CHOKWE
Figure 29 and Cover • Wood

King

Facial scarification, evident in this set, is a tradition shared by the Chokwe, Lundi, and Barotse (Lozi-speaking) peoples whose home is the western province of Zambia. The Castles are huts characteristic of western Zambia, although they can also be found in other parts of the country.

Zambia is shaped much like a kidney and, appropriate to its shape, is in the center of sub-Saharan Africa. I first drove through the capital, Lusaka, in 1949 when it was a sleepy country town. Before independence in 1964 the development was all in the copper belt to the north.

Los Angeles is a Sister City to Lusaka. The relationship has led to the exchange of delegations but not much else. We had several visits from President Kaunda and his huge entourage of political types. The cost of their traveling style would have paid for the building of a new school in Zambia.

In 1993, when I found this set in Lusaka, I also visited President Chiluba at State House. There I ran into Vernon Mwaanga who greeted me with, "Ned, I haven't seen you for twenty-some years." My answer was short: "Vernon, it is twenty-some years since you were foreign minister."

Mwaanga had prospered as a businessman during those years, but the ordinary Zambian had suffered more and more, with not much economic hope in sight. That is a surprising shame.

My study of operations at the American-owned Roan Antelope copper mine in 1952 led me to believe the promise of independence was bright. That's what I said when I subsequently taught at Harvard Business School. American students believed my optimism; foreign students expected the worst in terms of nationalization, labor disputes, failing agriculture, and a general deterioration of the economy. The foreigners were right and I was wrong.

--- ✦ ---

But no one would have thought that, forty years later, after two decades of independence, conditions would have deteriorated as much as they had. What was a corrupt disaster under Kaunda has become a more corrupt basket case under Chiluba, with a sky-rocketing AIDS epidemic that compounds the other social and economic problems. The disease is flowing from the city to the country with startling rapidity. (If one were of a macabre turn of mind, one might see the terrible prevalence of AIDS in Zambia reflected in the chess pieces.)

While watching Zambian ethnic dances in the floor show at the hotel where I was staying, I got into a conversation with the show's producer, Maggie Banda. She is really a teacher of teachers and unusually frank for an African woman. Her male and female dance troupe was just back from an exhibition in Germany. When discussing HIV, she said, "We had two who were positive, but we didn't take them abroad. Every week I lecture them about AIDS, hand out condoms, and tell the women what are the acceptable and what are the forbidden positions."

Zambia's general decline extended to the university, which I had seen at the time of independence and had assisted with grant allocation from a Ford Foundation program. At that time there were some excellent expatriate teachers. Several dozen Zambians were finishing their doctoral studies at leading universities in Europe and the States, prior to returning to their homeland. Today only a handful of "sixth rate expats" (to quote Mwaanga) remain on the teaching staff. The Zambian Ph.D.'s who returned to Lusaka have now left to teach for more money in neighboring countries.

ZIMBABWE
SHONA

Figure 30 • Gray and White Soapstone

U.S. Secret Service personnel stood guard against potential assassins as Los Angeles Police Department cars swept up to the back entrance of the California Club, red lights flashing. President Robert Gabriel Mugabe of Zimbabwe was hustled through the club kitchen and into a freight elevator. It was 1994. Mugabe was attending a dinner in his honor. I was one of the hosts.

Standing next to him in the elevator, I took the opportunity to ask if he remembered me from another dinner forty years earlier in the capital of Zimbabwe at the Jameson Hotel, the only hotel in the city which would admit blacks. He replied, "Well, I certainly remember the interracial group, and I did go to the hotel a number of times."

"The group included Hardwick Holderness and Barbara Tredgold, the governor-general's sister," I added. Mugabe smiled in recognition. He said, "And you were the young American."

He did not appear to be upset at the reminder of that time when he was thirty and soon to embark on a long stretch in detention. During that time he earned three degrees. He also became a national hero as a result of oppressive British policies that resulted in other heroes such as Nehru, Nkrumah, Kenyatta, and Banda.

Now President Mugabe, like many nationalist leaders in the liberation struggle, must try to create investments and jobs for his country. Zimbabwe art will go a long way to bring that country and its culture to the attention of the western world.

Stone carving goes back centuries in Zimbabwe (formerly Rhodesia). The stone walls of Great Zimbabwe date from the eleventh and twelfth centuries, and feature the large Zimbabwe bird. For many years local whites, out of prejudice and ignorance, tried to ascribe the origins of the stone work to the Phoenicians, to

Knight

the Ethiopians, to anyone except the Bantu-speaking ancestors of the Shona and Matabele peoples who now rule the country. A British government official's refusal to accept the Shona's ancestors as creators of the massive Zimbabwe stonework led to the destruction of Shona artifacts found during one excavation in the ruins in the late nineteenth century. Apparently the excavators hoped to find evidence of the Phoenicians farther down in the dig.

Subsequent excavations by archaeologists did prove the African origins of the site. Nonetheless, the prejudicial question of origin persisted well into the twentieth century. When living in Harare (then Salisbury) in 1952–53, I carried on a fierce correspondence in the press with far-right racists on the issue. One such protagonist, Lord Graham, a Scot, attempted to settle the argument by quoting an article in an old Encyclopedia Britannica. Rarely, at least in the heart of Africa, can one have the rejoinder: "That's out of date. Read *my* article in the more recent Encyclopedia Britannica."[2]

Today local craftsmen are attempting to rebuild the Zimbabwe ruins. No special technology is needed. They simply build hot wood fires on granite outcrops (*kopjes*, from the Afrikaans) and throw cold water along the cracks. The resulting pieces are then laboriously shaped to fit the ruins. Hundreds of thousands of building blocks must be replaced.

One day, in a less settled part of Zimbabwe, another site may be discovered that will provide more evidence of the early Shona stone workers and their gold mining, cattle raising, and agricultural activities.

Shona society was organized at a local level without a great chief or king. It was less hierarchical than the societies of Nguni peoples such as the Zulus and

their descendants in western Zimbabwe, the Matabele.[3] The Shona comprise the majority ethnic group in Zimbabwe.

Western accounts of the British conquest of the Shona often portray them as passive. But the Shona did resist fiercely, led not by a king but by a spiritual leader, Mbuya Nehanda, a remarkable and highly respected woman. I have an old print depicting her that suggests the inner strength she drew upon to resist the white invaders before her untimely execution at the hands of the British.

At the dinner for President Mugabe, I discussed Shona chess sets with him and ventured that, if I were designing a Shona set, the Queen would be the largest piece and would depict Nehanda. Mugabe agreed enthusiastically.

There was a hiatus in Shona stone carving that lasted some five hundred years. A noted French critic, Pierre Descargues, commented, "The Shona sculptors appeared to pick up their tools where their ancestors of several hundred years before had laid them down."[4] I'm not sure how to account for the hiatus. One explanation is advanced by Olivia Burdett-Coutts of Harare and Toronto, a connoisseur of Shona art. She suggests that, because of the deeply inherent identification of Shona art with Shona religion, the only "art" for many centuries was wooden objects that served useful or religious purposes. However, I feel that more needs to be learned about this long interruption in stone carving.

It isn't entirely politically correct in Zimbabwe today to highlight this hiatus. To do so appears to give too much credit to the "colonialist" Frank McEwen. It is ironic that, in 1956, when McEwen was invited to Rhodesia by the white community to help interject more *European* culture, he went hellbent to recognize and encourage the indigenous Shona sculptors.

While director of the National Museum, McEwen recruited carvers and created a market for Shona sculpture.[5]

Today there are galleries of Shona art in Harare, London, New York, and Los Angeles. The first museum breakthrough was in Paris at the Musee Rodin where McEwen had been a curator. The Smithsonian, despite its strength in ethnic art, does not yet have an example of Shona work.

The *Economist* said of the Shona: "The world's best unrecognized sculptors…are producing stonework…the finest some say in the world."[6] And Michael Shepherd, an English critic writing for the London *Sunday Telegraph*, has gone so far as to say that possibly five of the ten finest sculptors in the world come from the small band of Shona people.[7]

Basil Davidson deserves the lion's share of credit for persuading the outside world that Africa has produced some of the finest art known to man. His cascade of books on African history has illuminated the dark continent.[8] In the forty years since we first dined together in Harare, he has been a tower of liberal strength.

The first contemporary Shona master carver was Joran Marigi, a McEwen recruit, from the Nyanga district of Mutare (Umtali). One of his students, John Takawira, produced a magnificent serpentine sculpture that was presented to Queen Elizabeth by Zimbabwe at the time of independence. (A seventy-pound sculpture by Takawira is in my office; I know the weight well, because I carried it from Harare on a series of airplanes.)

Curiously, the first international impetus for the contemporary work of Shona soapstone artists came from the Rhodesian Central Intelligence organization. Desperate for hard currency, they made a collection of art and brought it to the United States to sell in exchange for dollars—this at a time the United States and most of the world had sanctions against Rhodesia.

In Los Angeles, San Diego, and Santa Barbara they were able to enlist the support of banks, stores, and scholars under the guise of promoting African art. Chess sets were being sold ostensibly on behalf of poor African artists oppressed by the Ian Smith government, to support black art behind the backs of the white authorities. The ploy was plausible for a while, but in the long run was proven a hoax. Although I found the antics suspicious, I did attend a large Bank of America cocktail party in Los Angeles debuting the Shona art. I wrote many articles about the Rhodesians' tricks and got a good grilling from the their CIA.

My good friend Dr. David Brokensha, a staunch liberal Democrat, accepted a number of handsome pieces of Shona art for the University of California, Santa Barbara, where he worked as an anthropologist, and for his private collection. It was with amazement that David and his companion opened the door of their home one morning to find FBI agents, with guns drawn, wanting to interrogate them about dealing in illicit Rhodesian art objects. Later the FBI dropped all charges. The Rhodesian mastermind was eventually arrested in Florida and prosecuted.

The Rhodesian CIA front man who came to Los Angeles had an early soapstone chess set, which I would have accepted as a gift or bought despite my suspicions. But he would not sell; he said he needed it for an exhibit in San Francisco. As a result, I received neither a Zimbabwe set nor an FBI visit.

Today the most prominent promoter of Shona sculpture is Anthony J. Ponter, a fourth-generation Zimbabwean, married to an American, who divides his time between the two countries. Ponter has worked tirelessly to encourage collectors to invest in Shona art. He has done well by doing good.

Who makes the greatest contribution to art? Some say it is the artist—in Zimbabwe, the sculptor working in his outdoor patio studio; others say it is the entrepreneur—like Ponter, who puts up the capital to buy the art (Ponter doesn't believe in consignments) and creates a market of collectors.

Ponter collaborated with Joan Travis, my longtime friend from Leakey Foundation days, to exhibit and sell Shona art at the Natural History Museum in Los Angeles. According to newspaper reports, the sales grossed over a quarter of a million dollars, with profits going to the museum and the artists.

The quality of my soft stone set does not match that of the larger, highly polished pieces produced by Zimbabwe sculptors and found increasingly in galleries of African art around the world.

As customary in African sets, the Castles are huts. Animals are eschewed; instead the Knight is a figure with a flat headdress and frowning countenance. The King wears the crown. The Queen is an African woman with stylized breasts, hands on hips.

ZIMBABWE

Figure 31 • Green and Yellow-Brown Soapstone

A different styles marks this set. The main pieces are similar except that the King carries a sword; and the Knight, who carries two knives laid back beside his head, is smaller than the Bishop. The Castles are mod-

Knight

eled after the great conical towers in the Zimbabwe Ruins south of the capital, Harare.

Originally called Salisbury, the capital was laid out by an American surveyor in the late nineteenth century. On my first visit in 1952, Salisbury reminded me of a small ranch town in Texas—farmers coming in on Saturdays for supplies, blacks living in a separate shanty town. And of course there were no skyscrapers then.

The origin of a similar set, owned by my friend Carol Patton, a relation of the general from Pasadena, became the subject of some dispute. Patton is an avid collector of Cecil John Rhodes material of all kinds; I have sold her books and letters pertaining to the former prime minister of the Cape Colony. (It was Rhodes who gave his name to the scholarships and Rhodesia, the former name of Zimbabwe.)

Patton acquired the chess set in question from someone who had been first secretary of the South African High Commission in London. The set was alleged to have come directly to his family from Cecil Rhodes himself. Patton was advised to insure the set for a high value because it purportedly came from Kenya and was rare.

In view of what I knew about the revival of Zimbabwe carving by Frank McEwen in the 1950s, I had a fairly clear idea of what to say to Patton when she sent me a photograph of the set and asked me to comment on its origin.

The set bears no resemblance to any known Kenya set. Furthermore, it could not be a Zimbabwe set owned by Rhodes because he died in 1902, half a century before Malawi carvers in Zimbabwe began to make such sets. For further confirmation, I contacted Dr. David Alexander, head of the Rhodes trust in the

United States. He knew of no reference to Rhodes and chess. In addition, Patton's research at Rhodes House in Oxford revealed no record of chess sets owned by Rhodes.

When I lived in Zimbabwe (then Rhodesia) in 1952–53, I did see small stone figures of animals in friends' homes, but never a chess set. They came later, long after Rhodes was lying under the flat stone slab in the Matopos Hills of western Zimbabwe.

Incidentally, a set Frank Greygoose identifies as Southern Rhodesian[9] is very much in the Malawi style and almost certainly was carved by a Malawian working in either Southern Rhodesia or Malawi.

ZIMBABWE

Figure 32 • Ebony and Ivory

Elephant poaching is rigorously suppressed in Zimbabwe. Rangers keep the elephant population healthy and growing. Zimbabwe ivory comes from elephants that die of natural causes. Proceeds from the sale of that ivory are used to pay the rangers' salaries.

Despite plundering by early European settlers, Zimbabwe has many riches besides ivory. Placer gold and copper mines existed from the days of Great Zimbabwe six hundred years ago.

You could even say that the country's riches are responsible for our being able to enjoy the talents of Lee Grant, the Hollywood actress and producer who was nominated for an Emmy in 1993.

Around the turn of the century, a Russian immigrant to Southern Rhodesia, Jack Rosenthal, had the proverbial faithful African servant. As the story goes, on his deathbed the retainer gave his employer a map of a gold mine. The map was authentic. Rosenthal realized a substantial sum. He sent $5,000—a great

deal of money in 1905—to a nephew who was living in a cold-water, walk-up tenement on New York's Lower East Side.

Years later, at the Benedict Canyon (Los Angeles) home of my friends Genevieve and Buddy Davis, I was introduced to Rosenthal's nephew's son, Abraham. He told me that his great-uncle's largesse had enabled his family to move to the Upper West Side. More importantly, it allowed Abraham to attend Julliard School and become a classical musician. His daughter also attended Julliard, but she was more interested in acting than in music.

Movie moguls seemed to have an antipathy to so-called Jewish names, even though many of them were Jewish themselves. Starlets fared better if they had Anglo-Saxon names. Abraham's daughter needed a stage name. He was thinking about this one day as he drove past Grant's Tomb.

"I thought Grant would be a good solid name," he said, "but some family members thought it might antagonize southerners to use the general's name." The solution was obvious: give the aspiring young actress the first name "Lee."

A coda to the story is that Lee Grant's daughter, also an actress, chose the stage name Dinah Manoff.

Pawn

Traditional Shona styles are represented in this set. The Knight is a drummer rather than an animal. The King is balding, a sign of wisdom much respected among the Shona. The Queen carries a child on her back, as do many women throughout rural Africa. The Pawns are exceptionally well carved.

Olivia Burdett-Coutts, the connoisseur of Shona art, dates this set as older than the other soapstone sets in my collection. She also believes it is artistically the best.

Queen

ZIMBABWE

Figure 33 • Green and Gray Soapstone

Style variations in Zimbabwe sets—whether of soapstone, serpentine, ebony, or ivory—reflect the diverse talents of the indigenous Shona carvers and visiting artists such as the Malawians. Even those sets that follow a standard design are rarely "airport art."

The relationship of this set to the three previously described Zimbabwe sets is hard to establish. I surmise that it was made in a different part of the country. The Castle is neither in the conventional African hut form nor in the distinctive pattern of the conical towers of Great Zimbabwe. The bare-breasted Queen with her hair in successive rolls and the King with his staff and scroll are, to the best of my knowledge, sui generis in Zimbabwe sets.

One similarity with the Shona set is notable: the use of unusually small heads for Pawns (¾ inch in this set, 1¼ inch in the Shona). Of course Pawns are expected to be smaller than other pieces, but in these two Zimbabwe sets the Pawns are disproportionately small.

BOTSWANA
!KUNG

Figure 34 • Clay

"Zucky" Schapera of the University of Cape Town coined the term *Khoisan* to differentiate the peoples known popularly and pejoratively as Bushmen and Hottentots from the Bantu-speaking groups such as the Nguni and Sotho who migrated to southern Africa at least 10,000 years after the Khoisan.

The San, a proper name for Bushmen, include the !Kung and a number of other ethnic groups, all of whom speak a click language. (There are remnants of

Pawn

peoples, such as the Hadza, speaking a click language in Tanzania, relics of a probable move from the north along the east coast of Africa perhaps twenty thousand years ago.) The short, yellowish-brown hunters and food gatherers occupied most of southern Africa before the coming of the Bantu-speaking black people in approximately the twelfth century. Now the San range across much of Botswana (formerly Bechuanaland) and into northern Namibia.[10]

To many observers the San posed a philosophical dilemma. Should they be encouraged to maintain their nomadic lifestyle with as little interference as possible? Or should they be enticed or forced into the lifestyle of the majority in Botswana, with its attendant schools, clinics, and taxes?

The issue was settled tragically for many San who were used as trackers by the South African army in the Angolan war, with its grave cultural consequences. The !Kung and other San peoples were torn from their traditional roots to fight in the South African war against the South Western Peoples Organization (SWAPO). Once SWAPO came into power, the San did not want to settle in Namibia. Many were moved to camps in Northern Cape Province, where they had no way of resuming their traditional lifestyle and found adaptation to farming the desolate land unsatisfactory. Without livestock, hunting areas, or even the traditional cereal foods, they drifted into drink and violence. It was a swift and tragic example of deracination.

Many San people live as virtual slaves of the Batswana and eke out an existence as cattle herders. Cattle are not part of the traditional San culture and, in fact, are a threat to it. There are more cattle than people in Botswana.

Much is still to be learned about the San peoples. For example, how did they acquire the high level of skill revealed in their prehistoric art work preserved in caves throughout South Africa, Lesotho, and Namibia? For a long time, the Picasso-like distortions of human figures in some of the San cave paintings were attributed to error. But when you understand that the work was done by shamans or religious figures under the influence of mind-altering drugs such as the strong, local marijuana, you find similarities to drawings produced today by people so influenced. Few artists, though, could match the San shamans in their physiological insight.

The African designer of this chess set has not done a good job of indicating the slender build of most San people or their yellowish-brown cast. The set does reflect the !Kung use of bows and poison-tipped arrows for hunting, and skins for clothing. The Castle is a hut that differs from those of Bantu-speaking people in that it does not have four walls or a thatch roof. The !Kung can pick up their possessions and move when weather or food supply dictates. They have been romanticized for their ability to survive in the vast Kalahari Desert. Even the widely shown film *The Gods Must Be Crazy*, based upon the landing of a Coca Cola bottle on a Bushman's head, has not ruined them.

NAMIBIA

SAN

Figure 35 • Metal

A modern sculptor's striking conception of the San peoples, this set was cast in bronze with copper nitrate (green) and ferro nitrate (brown and black) in 1988. It was made by the traditional lost wax process. The

sculptor, Guy du Toit, obtained the soft shell of cuttle fish from the Namibian coast. Like balsa wood, the shell is easily shaped; it was used to design the three-dimensional pieces. The backs of the Pawns show a vertical series of round dots, the actual impressions of cuttle fish vertebrae.

Ethnicity in this set reflects two quite disparate cultures, the San peoples of Namibia and of Botswana. Both groups are undergoing cataclysmic change. Their culture is a motif throughout the set. The Castle is sur-realistically depicted as vulnerable, with three San arrows going in one side and their points coming out the other. Du Toit reacted viscerally to the steely, mechanistic war technology used by South Africa and the often more militarily effective poison-tipped missiles from the bows of the San.

Du Toit is an Afrikaner—a South African of European ancestry who speaks Afrikaans. He completed his compulsory (for whites) military service in two years. His university career was thrice interrupted by his being involuntarily called up for "the border war" in Angola and to fight secretly in Rhodesia.

An early sign of his purification in the crucible of war was his refusal to bear arms. He acknowledges the greater price paid by conscientious objectors, but is proud to have been a medic, although he was as frightened under enemy fire as any rifleman. He said, "The contrast between the Bushmen and the Bushwar was real Joseph Conrad *Heart of Darkness* emotion."

In the long, boring periods of war, between those of sheer terror, du Toit turned to art. His mother was a potter, but he had not considered it as a career. After the army he taught art in Soweto for seven years. Teaching gave him pleasure, as well as expiation of sin. He fought successfully to free himself from the

Bishop

iron jaws of a racist and disastrous ideology, known simplistically by the shibboleth *apartheid*.

After more than forty years of semiannual visits to South Africa, I am not surprised that it is difficult now to find anyone who supported Dr. Verwoerd, the assassinated prime minister (from 1958 to 1966) who was a proponent of apartheid. Indeed, when dining with du Toit in Verwoerdburg, a new "town" outside Pretoria, we talked about how businessmen wanted to change the town's name to avoid the stigma of a man who had been an intellectual deity to Afrikaners just a short generation ago.

Today du Toit is one of the few South African sculptors who supports himself solely through his art sales. He lives on an abandoned chicken ranch, where his studio can be bitterly cold in winter. Almost all of his figures are larger than life-size, and are made on commission or sold to major corporations, municipalities, and a few individuals.

This chess set was never a commercial success. Du Toit says I was the first person to show enthusiasm about it. He only cast five sets; one sold commercially and the others went to relatives. He created a sixth set for me as a favor. It is unlikely that he will design anything as small as chess pieces again.

NAMIBIA
HIMBA-HERERO
Figure 36 • Clay

King

The Herero, a warrior people, have been a central force in Namibian history. Today they are outnumbered by the Ovambo of northern Namibia, who constitute just over one-half of the country's population.

The Himba are a sub-group of the Herero. The Kaokoveld, where most of the Himba and their cousins, the Chimba, live, is even drier than the rest of arid Namibia; its normal rainfall is not enough to sustain agriculture. Although the Himba are black, they are known as the Red Ocher people for the mixture of clay and butterfat they smear on their bodies to protect themselves against the dryness.

Because they are the most isolated of the Herero peoples, the Himba maintain their traditions. My longtime friend Dr. Beatrice Sandelowsky told me a story that provides insight into those traditions. Namibian by birth, Sandelowsky studied at the University of California, Berkeley for her Ph.D. and worked among the Himba. In 1982, when interviewing Kamasitu Tjipombo at Orumpembe, Sandelowsky asked him, through a translator, to name his parents.

"My father's name!" he said. Kamasitu reacted with shock and surprise because, as the translator explained, it was strictly forbidden to utter the name of one's father. "One of my relatives is here at Orumpembe. His name is Kenanimbi. He is my brother."

"Don't you ever mention the name of your father?"

"I can mention it. That's the one who gave birth to me."

Then, looking around to make sure no one else could be listening, Kamasitu said, "His name is Mitjavi Tjipembe."

"Do you know your age?" Sandelowsky asked.

"No, but I can guess. The year of my birth was the 'Year of Death.' Many cattle died that year. It was after the German war."

In 1951 I came to know the last great leader of the Herero, Chief Hosea Kutako. What a magnificent human being. What a panoramic life he led. On one occasion when I was ushered into his dignified presence in Windhoek, I felt as though I was shaking hands with history. Born in 1870, he participated in skirmishes against the Nama peoples to the south and fought against the ruthless German conquerors before World War I. Prussian Lieutenant General Von Trotha's infamous order to exterminate the Herero as vermin almost became a reality. Many Herero fled into neighboring Bechuanaland. It is said that their women refused to bear children who would be born into subjugated status. The birth rate fell to one percent.

And yet, some years ago at the moving, annual commemoration of the bitter war, I observed veterans of both sides amicably displaying the mutual respect of one warrior for another.

Another war, which took place before Kutako's time, had long fascinated me. It resulted in a rare and bitter defeat of the Herero by the Nama. In order to survive recrossing the arid Namib Desert, the overcome Herero were forced to drink the blood of scorpions. Hence the name: the Scorpion War. When I asked the regal chief about it, my lack of tact almost stopped the interview.

Chief Kutako led the South West African delegation to the United Nations to ask for independence for Namibia. Although he lived more than 100 years, he did not see his petition realized. Namibia did not achieve independence until 1990.

Kutako's chief lieutenant, Clemens Kapuuo, often took me to see his leader. Kapuuo also did not live to see his country's freedom. He was assassinated in his backyard by gunmen sent across the Angolan border by SWAPO. In retaliation the Herero attacked an Ovambo compound in Windhoek and killed a number of people who were supposedly SWAPO supporters. At their funerals I had to run for my life when gunfire broke out.

I haven't visited the Himba in recent years. Thus I was shocked to read in the December 1994 issue of *Condé Nast Traveler* that the village of Purros has become "some sort of Afro-theme park." From the magazine article I gleaned that an apparently well-intentioned plan initiated by the ethnologist Margaret Jacobsohn in the 1980s has gone awry. For about two years, small groups of tourists were flown into Purros to spend a few days learning about the Himba and their culture. In return, the Himba were given money on a per tourist basis and had the opportunity to earn more income by selling "ethnic trinkets." The hope was that the outside world would learn about the Himba's traditional ways without disrupting them.

However, because of the success of the tours, they multiplied—and became shorter in duration. No longer were tourists spending a leisurely few days learning about the Himba. Rather, they were flown in for only a few hours—just long enough to act like typical tourists, taking photographs and buying souvenirs. And the Himba accommodated. In response to the sound of the arriving plane, they gathered in a circle near their huts, with their wares for sale. According to the *Condé Nast Traveler* article, there was no longer "substantial interchange" nor "mutual respect" between cultural groups. Rather, what took place was "peddling" and "cultural contamination."

What a debacle. The failure of Jacobsohn's plan points up the problems inherent in attempting to share a culture with outsiders without polluting that culture in the process. Now Jacobsohn and Garth Owen-Smith, her colleague, are apparently trying to remedy the situation through talks with the Himba.

The chess set reflects the Himba cattle culture. If the set had been designed by me instead of by the sculptor

Joshua Ngenya, the Queen would not be wearing a rural field outfit. The Hereros closely copied German clothing styles of the 1890s, and have continued to dress in the same way. The women typically wear huge skirts with many petticoats, even in the hottest weather; blouses with Victorian, leg-of-mutton sleeves; and colorful kerchiefs piled high on their heads.

SAO TOME

Another One that Got Away

The scariest thirty minutes of my life took place on Sao Tome. While walking the two miles from a restaurant (where I had met with a local carver to negotiate the making of a chess set) to the *pousada* where I was staying, I was accosted by six, husky, young Portuguese men. They indicated through hand signals that they wanted to give me a lift. Instead of taking me to the pousada, they drove me to the edge of a large cliff overlooking the harbor and began performing gymnastics, signaling me to participate.

Suddenly, from behind, four of them grabbed my hands and feet and began swinging me over the cliff's edge. On each upswing I could see the waves beating the rocky shore some three hundred feet below. Just as suddenly as it began, the swinging stopped with a one-two-three motion. I felt one man let go of my arm. I waited for the fall. I really thought I was going to die.

Then I was standing up, numbed by the closeness of death.

They drove me to the pousada and, for the first time, I heard them speak English. They asked a rhetorical question: "You are leaving tomorrow?" I was. I did.

--- --- ---

Why did they want to scare me off their island? It was 1955. A fabric-covered biplane had taken me to Sao Tome, which is in the south Atlantic just west of Equatorial Guinea. My mission was to cover a political story for the American Universities Field Staff.

A revolution was brewing. Gardeners had been discovered sprinkling gasoline instead of water on the grass around the governor's mansion. The wooden structure was one match away from being destroyed. Army officers were among those being charged in the incident. They had managed to obtain a defense lawyer from Salazar's Portugal. The lawyer had been there several weeks.

When I arrived, the pousada was overbooked, and I had no choice but to share a room with him. There I was: an inquisitive and exceedingly rare (in those days) American visitor, with a typewriter, seemingly consorting with the officers' attorney. The secret police were not pleased by my presence. Innocence is not always a valid defense. ▨

Figure 1a: Uganda • Ceramic • The Kabaka, Then (circa 1890) side • King 4½ inches

Bishop

Figure 1b: Uganda • Ceramic • The Kabaka, Now side • King 4½ inches

King

Figure 2: Kenya • Luo • Kisii Stone • King 5 inches

Figure 3: Kenya • Animals • Kisii Stone • King 5¾ inches

Figure 4: Tanzania • Maasai • Wood • King 5 inches, Knight 5½ inches

Bishop

Figure 5: Malawi • Wood • King 3 inches

Figure 6: Malawi • Ebony and Red-painted Bone • King 3½ inches

Figure 7: Malawi • Black and Green Serpentine • King 4½ inches

Figure 8: Malawi • Ebony and Red Wood • King 3⅝ inches

Figure 9: Madagascar • Merina vs. Sakalava • Cattle Horn • King 3⅞ inches

Sakalava Castle

Figure 10: Madagascar • Merina • Wood • King 4½ inches

Pawn

Figure 11: Mozambique • Makonde • Mphingo and White Hardwood • King 6 inches

Figure 12: Mozambique • Yellowwood and Ebony • King 5½ inches, Queen 6 inches

Queen

Figure 13: Benin • Glazed Ceramic • King 5½ inches, Bishop 6½ inches

Figure 14: Maunoury's Faux Chess Set • King 4 inches

King

King

Figure 15: Senegal • Cast Brass • King 4 inches, Knight 4½ inches

Mende Knight

Figure 16: Sierra Leone • Creoles vs. Mende • Wood • King 3¼ inches, Creole Pawn 3⅝ inches

Figure 17: Ivory Coast • Baoule • Resin and Wire • King 6 inches

Figure 18: Burkina Faso • Iron • King 2½ inches, Knight 3 inches

Queen

Figure 19: Mali • Gold and Black Metal • King 4¼ inches

Figure 20: Ghana • Ashanti • Gold Weights • King 2¾ inches

King

Figure 21a: Nigeria • Yoruba vs. Hausa • Thornwood • Hausa side • King 2¾ inches

Yoruba Bishop

Figure 21b: Nigeria • Yoruba vs. Hausa • Thornwood • Yoruba side • King 2½ inches

Pawn

Figure 22: Nigeria • South • Thornwood • King 4 inches

Figure 23a: African-European • Grass Skirts • Porcelain • African side • King 3¼ inches

Figure 23b: African-European • Porcelain • European side • King 3¼ inches

Figure 24: Chad • Wood • King 5¾ inches

Figure 25: Zaire • Ivory • King 3 inches

Queen

Figure 26: Congo • Wood, Burlap, and Chicken Feathers • King 3½ inches

King

Figure 27: Congo • Ebony and Ivory • King 4⅛ inches

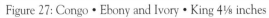

Figure 28: Angola • Perforated Ivory and Ebony • King 3⅛ inches

King

Figure 29: Zambia • Chokwe • Wood • King 3¾ inches

Figure 30: Zimbabwe • Shona • Gray and White Soapstone • King 3 inches

Figure 31: Zimbabwe • Green and Yellow-Brown Soapstone • King 3¼ inches

Figure 32: Zimbabwe • Ebony and Ivory • King 5¼ inches

Figure 33: Zimbabwe • Green and Gray Soapstone • King 3¼ inches

Figure 34: Botswana • !Kung • Clay • King 2½ inches

King

Figure 35: Namibia • San • Metal • King 2½ inches

Castle

Figure 36: Namibia • Himba-Herero • Clay • King 2⅝ inches

Queen

Queen

Figure 37a: South Africa • Painted Wood, Plastic, Cloth • Coloured side • King 6⅛ inches

Queen

Figure 37b: South Africa • Painted Wood, Plastic, Cloth • Malay (Muslim) side • King 6⅛ inches

Figure 38: South Africa • Shy Pawns • Resin • King 3 inches

Figure 39a: South Africa • Khoi Khoi, Dutch • Glazed Ceramic • Khoi Khoi side • King 5 inches

Bishop

Figure 39b: South Africa • Khoi Khoi, Dutch • Glazed Ceramic • Dutch side • King 5 inches

King

Bishop

Figure 40: South Africa • Nguni • Composition • King 3 inches

Bishop

Figure 41: South Africa • Zulu • Ivory • King 5¾ inches

Queen

Figure 42a: South Africa • Ndebele vs. Zulu • Composition and Wood • Zulu side • King 4 inches

Figure 42b: South Africa • Ndebele vs. Zulu • Composition and Wood • Ndebele side • King 3½ inches

Queen

Figure 43: South Africa • Ndebele • Clay • King 2½ inches

Queen

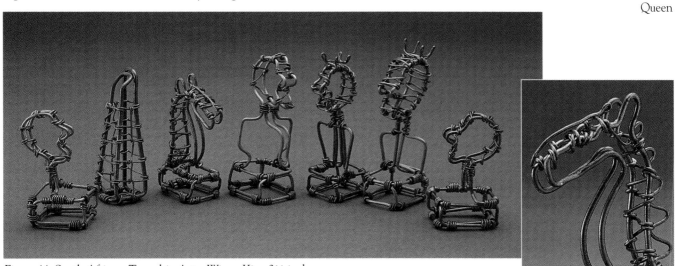

Figure 44: South Africa • Township Art • Wire • King 3¼ inches

Knight

Figure 45: South Africa • Animals • Ivory • King 3 inches

Figure 46a: South Africa • Pondo • Porcelain • King 3½ inches

Figure 46b: South Africa • Sotho • Porcelain • King 3½ inches

Figure 46c: South Africa • Zulu • Porcelain • King 3½ inches

Figure 46d: South Africa • Xhosa • Porcelain • King 3½ inches

Queen

Figure 47: Swaziland • Porcelain • King 3½ inches

Bishop

Figure 48: Swaziland • Green and Black Stone • King 2¾ inches

Figure 49: Swaziland • Pewter • King and Queen 2¾ inches

Bishop

Figure 50: Lesotho • Moshoeshoe I • Silver • King 2½ inches

Detail

Figure 51: Tristan da Cunha • Wood, Postage Stamps, Painted Designs • King 3⅛ inches

S O U T H E R N   A F R I C A

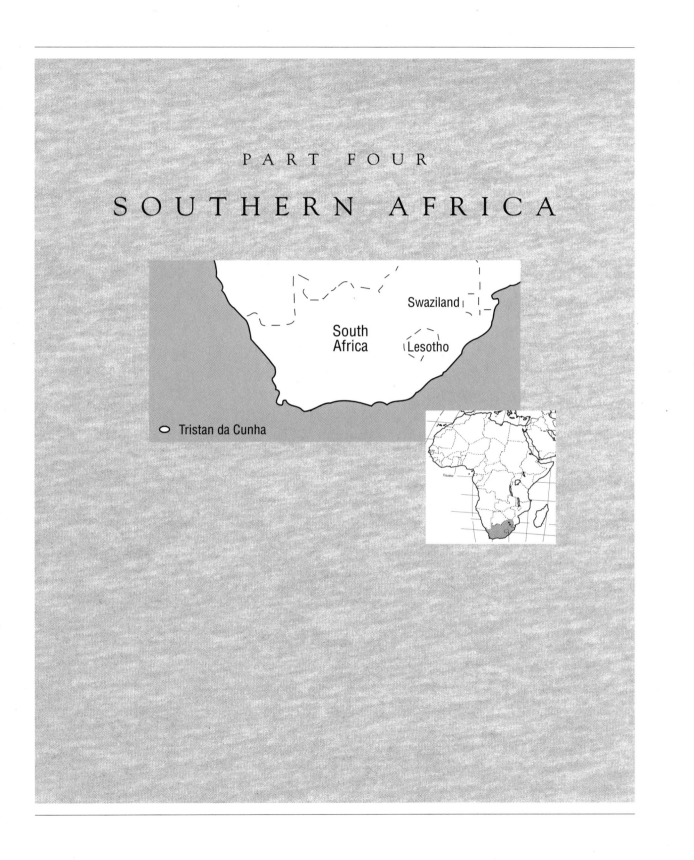

Swaziland

South
Africa

Lesotho

Tristan da Cunha

SOUTH AFRICA
COLOURED VS. MALAY (MUSLIM)
Figures 37a and 37b • Painted Wood, Plastic, Cloth

"There is a lovely road that runs from Ixopo into the hills. These hills are grass-covered and rolling, and they are lovely beyond any singing of it."

So starts Alan Paton's novel *Cry, the Beloved Country.*[1] The book so moved me that, at one time, I could recite the first chapter from memory. When it was being made into a film in 1950, Paton invited me to visit the location where it was being shot—his brother-in-law's farm at Ixopo (pronounced with a Xhosa click on the *x*). There, Paton introduced me to Canada Lee, who played the black lead, supported by a young Sydney Poitier.

Lee's uncle, a merchant mariner, had stopped often enough in Cape Town to father a family—people Lee had never met. We agreed to go together a few days later to try to find them. A taxi took us to what were then the dirt roads of Athlone, one of the lower-middle-class Coloured suburbs of Cape Town.

We knocked on the door of the correct "stand number." Two young Coloured faces appeared behind cautiously lifted lace curtains and stared at us with apprehension. Perhaps they saw the white man as a representative of some evil authority and the huge black man as "the bad black man coming to get them," as in their mother's frightening bedtime stories.

We knocked and knocked. Finally the door opened a crack, revealing two shy girls of about sixteen and seventeen. They spoke no English; Lee spoke no Afrikaans. My few words of Afrikaans were our only linguistic bridge.

Once it was established that Lee and the girls were, in fact, cousins, we were invited into the parlor for *rooibos* (red bush) tea. Thus began forty-odd years of visits to friends in Athlone.

So I felt somewhat at home in 1995 drinking tea with artist Tyrone Appollis in his tiny living room as we engaged in the first of several lengthy discussions, both there and over lunch at the five-star Mount Nelson Hotel, about the making of a chess set.

At age 37, Appollis had already exhibited in South Africa, Switzerland, Germany, and Paris. Not only does he produce work in wood, cloth, and other materials, such as in this set; he also paints in oil, has published a number of poems, and has quite a reputation as a performer on the penny whistle.

Coloured • King

Malay • King

An aside to my "Malay" friends: Today, it is not politically correct to use ethnic terms in describing Malays. Many deny being Malays; they want to be called Muslim, without regard to their historical background. I accept their chosen orientation. However, this chess set represents a centuries-old historical division in the Western Cape, and it should be considered in that historical context.

The Malay King represents the famous Malay religious leader Sheikh Joseph, whose tomb lies between Cape Town and Somerset West. The Malay Queen wears a scarf, a *medora*. Although it is rare today to see a woman in the streets completely covered, the medora is still common among Muslim women.

The Castle is a mosque. An unusual feature of the Malay side is that the Bishops and Pawns both represent imams. On the Pawns, Appollis imaginatively used red caps from toothpaste tubes to serve as what foreigners would call fezzes but are known on the Cape as *kufia*.

The Malay Knight is also unusual in that it represents a ship rather than a horse or some other animal—a ship that played an important role in the history of the Cape Malays. The Confederate raider *Alabama*, technically out of Mobile, Alabama, was built and commissioned in England and carried a crew that was largely English, not American southerners. Under the command of an American captain, Raphael Semmes, it scoured the Atlantic capturing and often sinking dozens of Union ships. From time to time the *Alabama* would come into Cape Town for provisions. The grave of one of its first officers can be found on the road just north of Cape Town.

Above a picturesque part of old Cape Town once known as the Malay Quarter, and now being restored, is Lion's Head ridge. In the days of the American Civil War, the young and the curious would climb up to Lion's Head early in the morning for the best view of the South Atlantic, stretching out to the north and west. At the first sighting of the *Alabama*'s familiar sails, the cry would go up: "*Daar kom die Alabama, die Alabama kom oor die see.*" And so was born the ditty well known to the peoples of the Western Cape and indeed to most South Africans.

The Coloured side of the set is led by a famous figure in South African history: Willem Adriaan van der Stel, who succeeded his father Simon as governor in 1699. Willem, as King, sports his high Dutch hat and mustache. A little-known fact about the early governor is that, although he represented the Dutch aristocracy, he had every claim to be Coloured. His mother was from India and quite dark complexioned. Of course in the days of apartheid this was not taught to Afrikaner (white) school-children any more than the fact that President Paul Kruger, the great Boer hero, had Coloured ancestry.

The Queen is outfitted in a long, colorful dress traditionally favored by the Coloured community.

The Bishop wears a mitre and ecclesiastical dress. The Cape's long history of horse racing and the notable successes achieved by Coloured jockeys are represented in the Knight. A brick house with corrugated iron roof, typically found in low-income neighborhoods, stands for the Castle. The Pawns are Coloured workers.

The American press never gets "Coloured" straight, perhaps because of the complexities involved in the term and a lack of familiarity with South African culture. For a while in the early 1990s journalists used the term *so-called Coloured*, which was politically correct then but is now passé. The terms *mixed*, which has pejorative overtones, and *mulatto* may be appropriate in certain instances in the United States, but they are not part of the African culture. And mulatto does not fit the people of South Africa at all.

In the late seventeenth century there were no "black Africans" within several hundred miles of Cape Town. When the Dutch established their station in 1652 there were local people whose appearance and culture were quite different from the Xhosa or Zulu peoples who now form the second largest population in the Western Cape—outnumbered only by the Coloured people who constitute a majority of Cape Town's population. And there were about eight Khoi Khoi groups.

There is no short way to describe the complex ancestry of the six million Coloured people in South Africa. They are descended from the yellowish-brown-skinned Khoi Khoi people; the Malay people brought from Java; the black Nguni peoples—mostly Xhosa—who migrated to the Western Cape from the Transkei and from other areas in the east and north where Bantu languages are spoken; the Dutch,

French, and English settlers; and the many crews of passing vessels of all nationalities.

In a paper describing his work in genetics M. C. Botha, a University of Cape Town professor, wrote:

> My study proves that the Coloured have 36% southern African blood, while we whites have 7%. Therefore the Coloured people have only 29% more Coloured blood than we have. So where is the big difference between us? Is 29% sufficient to divide into different races? I think not. The fact is that the Coloured people are just a little less pure than we are.[2]

For a time in the 1960s, the Coloured elite chose to speak only English. In the 1980s they called themselves black, as if to unite themselves with black Africans in a common struggle. But to call the Coloured black is as culturally and racially incorrect as it would be to call all the Latino peoples of the United States black. It creates a false unity that breaks down by place of origin, by religion, by language, and by a thousand other criteria.

Given their subordinate position in society, it is no wonder the Coloured had such low self-esteem in the past. And it is understandable that they suffered from alcoholism, wife beating, incest, tuberculosis, and illiteracy—problems that the whites appeared to rise above. But talk to an old Afrikaner who will be honest with you, and he will tell you that the Afrikaners of the Cape in the 1930s had all the same problems. It was for good reason that the major sociological study of South Africa in that decade was the Carnegie Corporation report on poor whites.

Because of the severe conditions the Coloured people faced in the first half of this century, there was a lot of "passing" or, in the vernacular, "trying for white." It was not hard for a young Coloured woman with light skin to hie herself off to the Transvaal, where there were almost no Coloured people, claim Portuguese origin, and obtain a job as a secretary. Studies of the Cape Coloured suggest that there were about one million light-skinned Coloured people missing from the base population.

The most succinct way of describing Coloured people was told to me in 1983 by David Curry, chair of the Coloured Labour Party. He said, "You can truly put a label on us: 'Made in South Africa.'"

And so, in a way, are the Afrikaners. Professor Pieter Grobbelaar of Stellenbosch University once said to me, "Altogether fifty percent of our legends, folk songs, and poems in Afrikaans come from the Coloured people."

There are several groups of Coloured people who are not represented in this chess set. For example, the Coloured people of the Transvaal, small in numbers, have quite a different history from that of the Kaapenaars or Cape Coloured people. I have lived among them in the Transvaal. One of them is my lovely goddaughter, now in high school. But they are not included in the set because they are not Cape Coloured.

The "Bastards" of Rehoboth in Namibia also are not represented. Actually, they refuse to be called Coloured and will indignantly correct a stranger, saying, "Man, Ek is nie kleuring nie, Ek is'n baster." Better to be a proper bastard of presumed Hottentot and German genes than a Coloured (kleuring). When I spoke at the dedication of a small museum in Rehoboth, I saw and heard the people's pride in having a proper baster institution.

Although Coloured in origin, the Griqua people in what is now called the Eastern Cape are not part of this set. They split off from the Western Cape and, for a time, formed their own nation, Griqualand. When I visit their one-time capital, Kokstad, I think of the days when Adam Kok was the *kaptein* or head of the government. One of my proudest possessions is the original six-page letter, dated March 12, 1850, from Kok in Phillipolis to the editor of the *South African Commercial Advertiser* protesting the Orange River Sovereignty Proclamation. The great Griqua leader was illiterate, but he placed his large X in the space next to his name provided by the person who wrote the letter for him.

This set also does not include what are known in Natal to this day as Dunn's People. They are the descendants of an Englishman and his Zulu consorts; they even formed their own Zulu regiment. But they are markedly different from the Cape Coloured, and they lack the cosmopolitan ethnicity of the Capetonians. Physically, Dunn's People have no Khoi Khoi or Malay traces; culturally, they do not speak Afrikaans and do not belong to a Dutch Reformed Church.

Who, then, *is* the set about? The title is "Coloured vs. Malay." The two groups have been distinct entities—although not without exchanging genes along the way—for two hundred years. The major difference between them is that the South African Malays are Muslim, as true Malays are; whereas nearly all the Cape Coloured are Christian, the majority belonging to the main Dutch Reformed Church (*Nederduits Gereformeerde*).

If the term *Malay* ever had a justification, it was to distinguish those South Africans whose antecedents were the artisans brought from Java by the Dutch East India Company. They contributed richly to the cui-sine, architecture, language, and myriad other aspects of South African culture.

The Cape Coloured and Malays spoke what came to be known as *kombuis taal* (kitchen language), which differed from High Dutch and gradually evolved into the official Afrikaans language. These Malays and the handful of Cape Coloureds who had converted to the Muslim religion could not read Arabic.

Not surprisingly, then, the first book published in Afrikaans was the Koran, printed in Turkey for the Malays in the Cape. In 1862 the Cape Town Muslim Theological School was established by Abubakr Effendi and others who had been sent there by the Turkish sultan. The school published Abubakr's book *Demonstration of the Religious Practice of Islam*, in which he says he came 15,000 miles to learn the Dutch language so that he could teach religion to the Cape Malays and lead them away from non-Koranic practices.[3] His granddaughter Kermé Sinclair, who has proudly kept her Turkish culture, lives in Plumstead with her physician husband, a Scots Muslim. When I dined in their home recently they gave me an Arabic-English translation of the original book.

Over the years, the distinction of the Malays as a group has become hopelessly confused, to the point that today there is almost no difference between them and the Coloured in terms of ethnic origin. The distinctions have been blurred by more than one hundred years of intermarriage: Malays and the Bantu-speaking Africans in the last century; Malays and Muslims of Indian and Pakistani extraction, with the creation of new kinds of extended families, many with close ties between the Muslim Indians in Cape Town and Durban, Natal on the east coast of South Africa; Malays and the Coloured population of the Cape, with its own Khoi Khoi and European background.

Also, in the last decade there has been considerable outmarriage of Muslim (Malay) women with men of European origin, a practice that has become even more prevalent now that it is legal. Some attribute the increase in such unions to greater opportunities for those married women in business and academia; others consider the increase insignificant and the mention of it to be in poor taste.

In any case, for all of the reasons cited above, in South Africa today the major difference between the Muslims, who used to be called Malays, and the Coloured people is religion.

Unfortunately, there are hundreds of instances in which Africans or whites try to make buffoons of Coloured people. I resent every one of them. Perhaps the most egregious example was the treatment of the Hottentot Venus in the eighteenth century. Because of her elephantine buttocks, she was taken to Europe by whites and exhibited as a freak in countless fairs. (Yes, the steatopygia of the Khoi Khoi is evident in some Coloured people in Cape Town.) She was displayed in the nude so that her genitalia could be examined by the salacious. Eventually, stripped of all dignity and humanity, she drifted into prostitution and alcoholism and died without ever returning to the Cape.

In the nineteenth century the idea of the American minstrel show was quickly adapted by the Cape Coloured community. I refuse to watch the annual Coon Carnival when it marches through the streets of Cape Town. It has become a lower class phenomenon and a source of great controversy in the Coloured community; many leaders and members of the middle class see it as degrading. Of course not all black carnivals are demeaning. I attended the

Caribbean Carnival in London with a Zulu woman, and neither one of us found it in the least objectionable. But neither of us could accept the Coon Carnival because it reinforces a clownish, shuffling, subservient, feckless image of the Coloured man—an image that stands in sharp contrast to the thousands of educated Coloured people whose lives would be a credit to any community and who are, except for color, indistinguishable from the successful blacks and whites.

The Coon Carnival has been touted as an example of cooperation between the straights and moffies (South African slang for gays). A recent carnival king was a transvestite. But the Cape does not need the carnival as a show of tolerance. Indeed there are few places in all the world more accepting of different sexual orientations. In this respect Cape Town shares the honors with San Francisco.

Despite the fact that Coloured members have long sat on the Cape Town city council—and black members too, now—white attitudes toward Coloured people have not changed much with the end of apartheid. Before Tyrone Appollis agreed to make this chess set for me, I mentioned to a white art dealer, who exhibits work by Coloured artists, that I wanted a set to reflect the Coloured and Malay communities. She immediately said, "Of course it can be based on the Coon Carnival." When I suggested that would be offensive to many Coloured people, she replied, "Not at all. The Coloured people love the Coons performing."

When I was staying with the author Alan Paton at his place in Hillcrest, Natal in 1988, we had a conversation about how the Coloured people in Natal and the Free State differed from those in Cape Town. I had criticized his second novel *Too Late the Phalarope*[4] because in it he did not delineate the Afrikaner with the same insight he brought to his descriptions of the Zulu and English characters in *Cry, the Beloved Country.* I said the fault was in his lack of appreciation of the mutual interdependence of the Afrikaners and Coloured.

Consider: In the eighteenth century a group of Boers (Afrikaner farmers) decided to escape the hated British rule and trekked to Angola. After a century of living off the land beyond any government's control, they decided to return to South Africa. All sorts of vicissitudes befell them until, finally, a Coloured man named Will Jordaan took over their leadership and, like Moses, led them safely back to the promised land. (Now *there* would be a King for a chess set.)

Understand that Paton was the standard bearer of liberalism among the white English-speaking South Africans.[5] As we talked, I used the expression *bruin* (brown) *Afrikaners* and mentioned *ons bruin mense* (our brown people)—an expression frequently used by Afrikaners themselves, sometimes affectionately but more often patronizingly. Paton said he had no interest in including Coloured people as Afrikaners. He explained that he knew little about them because they did not live in Natal and he really only saw them on visits to Cape Town. And yet that evening, as the candles flickered and the bottle was drained, he displayed a kind of visceral identification with the Cape Coloured.

It was not until I read Peter Alexander's fine biography that I realized Paton had a penchant for Coloured prostitutes, which he apparently often indulged when in Cape Town.[6] Some reviewers of the biography emphasized the contrast of Paton's strong sexual drive and his strong beliefs as an Anglican. I would conjecture that Paton expected anonymity in Cape Town, many miles from where he was a public figure. He probably would not feel as vulnerable as he might with a black hooker on the waterfront in Durban, nor fear the chance of repercussion as much. In his autobiographical writings Paton says his rare but serious amorous relationships with white women caused him considerable moral consternation.[7]

I wish he were still alive so we could talk about this. But that evening in 1988 I was struck by his fascination with Coloured women in Western Cape. Somewhat out of character, he asked me whether I had ever had a close woman friend in that community. When I said yes, I sensed that he wanted the conversation to take a sexual, if not salacious, turn. But at that moment his wife Anne came in with late night tea, and the conversation came to a full stop.

⸻

Those of you who know South Africa will recognize that Tyrone Appollis has created his collage as a deliberate caricature of his people. It is redolent of Cape Town's famous District Six, a primarily Coloured residential area with a bohemian flavor, contiguous to the city center.

One of Prime Minister Verwoerd's cruelest actions as the architect of apartheid, and one I personally argued with him about until he threw me out of his office, was the forced removal of the people of District Six more than a generation ago. Except for the churches and mosques, which remained lonely sentinels, the land was bulldozed.

A most damning indictment of apartheid at the time was made by a leading Afrikaner poet, who paraphrased the story of the Christ child: the three wise men come from the desert-like Karoo and find the infant "met die sink 'n die sak van Distrik Ses"—in a poor hovel, with a corrugated iron roof and walls made of burlap sacks. The child is *brown*.

Only now, in happier days, is District Six being rebuilt, without racial restrictions. Hence there is a nostalgic quality to Appollis's chess set.

Leaders of the Coloured and Malay communities then and now are not represented in the set. They include men such as Richard Rive, who wrote the biography of Olive Schreiner; Peter Philander, the first Coloured poet to win the coveted Hertzog Prize for his work in Afrikaans; and my friend of fifty years, Dick van der Ross, the first person of color to head a so-called apartheid institution. He was honored by being selected as the sixth "Freeman" in Cape Town's three-hundred-year history.[8]

Without the buffoonery, a political Coloured chess set might have as King a radical of the 1940s such as my friend Benny Kies, or one of the leaders of the world's third largest Trotskyist party, which was based in Cape Town. A modern Coloured King would be Dr. Franklin Sonn, currently the South African ambassador in Washington. Dr. Abdurahman, politically active in 1903 and a longtime member of the city council, would be the Malay King.

But a political set was not Appollis's objective. Instead, he has succeeded brilliantly in reflecting the colorful qualities of a folk society that still exists.

SOUTH AFRICA
SHY PAWNS
Figure 38 • Resin

For the gay community in South Africa, Cape Town is a mecca similar to San Francisco in the United States. John Biccard, the Afrikaner who designed this set, lives on the bluff between Cape Town and Cape Point, in a quiet coign of vantage overlooking Atlantic Ocean beaches.

His cliffhanging residence is just a turn of the road from the suburb called Camps Bay, where Mary Renault—the author of novels based on ancient Greece, such as *The Persian Boy*—lived with her companion Julie Mullard. At one time, Renault and I played chess there regularly, with Mullard kibitzing more than I thought reasonable.

There wasn't much to suggest that Delos Cottage was the home of one of the best-selling novelists of the century. But, from viewing Renault's lovely garden, you got a clue to her novels. One flower bed sported a bronze statue of Hermes, much worn by the powerful storms of countless Cape winters. Originally, there was a fig leaf on the statue. Non-Victorian that she was, Renault had a workman remove it with a hacksaw. It had covered nothing! Not to be stuck with a Hermes-Aphrodite, Renault had the workman construct an organ of the right gender. It was entirely too priapic and not in proportion with the statue, but at least it was not Victorian.

There is a wonderfully whimsical quality to this set. Details indicated by black lines on the pieces reveal a dour King with downturned mouth, a coy Knight batting his eyes, a witch-like Queen, and terribly shy Pawns hiding behind their shields. Biccard personally supervises the molding of these sets, which have not yet been for sale outside of the major South African cities.

He showed me a gay chess set that he will never market. At first glance, the Pawns appear to have penises coming from beneath their clothing; in fact, they are swords. If the Biccard set ever got together with the Renault statue, there would be even more reason to call the suburb Camps Bay.

Pawn

SOUTH AFRICA
KHOI KHOI, DUTCH
Figures 39a and 39b • Glazed Ceramic

Khoi Khoi • Queen

Dutch • Bishop

This set was designed in great detail and historical accuracy by a remarkable young woman, Gabeba Abrahams, a member of the professional staff of the Cultural Museum of South Africa in Cape Town. She is the acknowledged world expert on life at the Cape of Good Hope in the seventeenth and early eighteenth centuries. Her pioneering study included a magnificent set of map overlays of Cape Town at the early stage of its development.[9]

More recently Abrahams has made a definitive study of the porcelain and pottery of the early Cape and has done research in museums in England, Holland, and the United States. She has also done considerable digging in Cape Town itself.[10]

When I was president of the Leakey Foundation, I wanted to extend our support of indigenous archaeologists in other parts of Africa to those in South Africa.[11] Abrahams was the most promising young person I could find in South Africa who was *not*—and there is no escaping the word—white. Of course she cannot properly be called "indigenous" because everyone in South Africa came from somewhere else. Even the Khoi Khoi migrated from eastern Africa several thousand years ago.

In the new South Africa one avoids ethnicity; it was such a deep, painful, and divisive force during the first forty years of my association with that country. Fortunately, legal race classification has been abolished in South Africa—a step the United States has yet to achieve. When Abrahams's son Mikhail was born, he was not registered as belonging to any particular race. But when Abrahams was growing up, her family was classified as Malay. At

one point Abrahams was nominal head of the Malay Museum.

There were about eight Khoi Khoi groups in the Cape in the 1600s, all of whom have lost their identity for various reasons, including genocide. One of the most prolific researchers on genetics of the early Cape is Henry Bredekamp at the University of the Western Cape. He is unusual in that he grew up near the old mission station of Genadendal where a Khoi Khoi group had been protected by the missionaries until gradually absorbed into the Coloured population. Bredekamp has distinct Khoi Khoi features; he tells how, as a boy, he was discriminated against and called derogatory names such as "Hotnot" by the average Coloured person. At the time, most of his contemporaries were boasting about a German grandmother or a Scottish grandfather. It is highly indicative of a new attitude and new self-image in the Cape that one of Bredekamp's students asked him hopefully, "Don't I look a little Khoi Khoi?"

This chess set was four years in gestation. It represents a great deal of research by Abrahams. There were difficulties in determining the ordinary dress of the time. Her elaborate drawings for the design took almost a year to create. Then began our lengthy search for a talented carver. We looked as far afield as Malawi without success. Finally, when we saw Rae Goosen's prize-winning chess set, we approached her with our plans.

Goosen lives in Plumstead, some twenty miles outside of Cape Town. In 1992 she won the Rupert Art Foundation prize for what the award cited as her "extraordinary sculptural piece *War Game*, a coffee table-size chess set, combining a group of handbuilt raku and pit-fired tiles and chess pieces." Later the same year she won the Cape Regional Exhibition. She has also exhibited her work in Taiwan. Here is what she wrote to me about her work:

> The integration and interaction of surface quality with form in my experimentation becomes significant. I use press-molding techniques to create textural qualities and I try to achieve the impression of antiquity through subdued patination, which results from pit-firing and refiring in an oxidized kiln numerous times.
>
> I achieve the final result through a convergence of technique and emotional response to the image, which may have undergone a number of processes. My work starts at a simple/technical level, and as it develops it grows into something much deeper, probably revealing more of me as a person.

Another reason the production of the set took so long was that Abrahams had definite ideas about colors and glazes, and the artist naturally had her own interpretations. In addition, there were technical problems in the mold-making and in assembling the pieces.

Here is Abrahams's description of the set, from a letter written to me:

> Digging up the tactile evidence of the 17th century Cape, the archaeological material remains of those early days of contact between the Dutch VOC incumbents and the indigenous Khoi, is a thrilling experience. Setting the stage through a chess set enhances this experience with the three-dimensional introduction of the players—the meeting of two completely different worlds. What was it really like? The defiant postures of the pieces speak for themselves. The regal kings and queens dominate the scene, and the pawns are belittled, very human, dressed in period costume guarding the front.
>
> Relations between the Dutch and the Khoi were sometimes amicable, sometimes hostile. Soon after

the Dutch settled, the Khoi realized that their presence was to be permanent, and their protests became more bitter, violent, and frequent. The first Dutch-Khoi war was fought in 1659.

> The design of the pieces is based on historical evidence, with artistic license. The details of the clothing come from archival sources, whereas the simplification, final glazing and color coordination were selected mainly for aesthetic purposes.
>
> Historical information for the Khoi pieces was more difficult to obtain than that for the Dutch. This is most unsatisfactory, and shows the bias of the research work which has placed an emphasis on the Dutch. The source material is mainly 17th and 18th century illustrations, as well as 19th century depictions by Samuel Daniel in the Africana Museum. The earlier sources are often subjective Europeanized versions, sometimes painted by artists who never visited the Cape. Therefore, the Khoi pieces are my personal interpretation, given these limitations.
>
> The Khoi dress is elegant in its simplicity, and creates a sense of warmth and comfort, with the draped animal skins. The natural textures and accessories such as feathers and shells combine with the yellow skin tones, and blend with nature. The more formal dress of the 17th century Dutch is dark and somber, with contrasting tones of black, white and gray, showing the Puritanical influence. The light fabrics are cottons and linens, and the darker shades are velvets, silks, satins and woolens. The Dutch adorned their dress with bows, ruffles, frills, laces, tassels and feathers.
>
> The Dutch king is portrayed by Jan van Riebeeck, first commander of the Cape of Good Hope in 1652, from the famous and controversial portrait by D. Craey in the Rijksmuseum, Amsterdam. The king is fashionably dressed in lace collar and cuffs, an ornamental buckled sash, and a plumed hat. His hair falls

in loose waves to his shoulders, and he bears the royal staff.

The Dutch queen, Maria de la Quellerie, first wife of van Riebeeck, is based on another Craey portrait. Her dress is the restrained good taste of the day. She wears the matron's coif, with a headpiece encircled with pearls, and matching eardrops. Her kerchief of fine linen, lawn or gauze, is flawlessly arranged.

The Khoi king is a regal figure based on 17th century drawings, with the facial features of Sandile, paramount chief of the Rharhabe in 1840. His reign was characterized by his resistance to the growing pressures of European encroachment. He was involved in the seventh, eighth and ninth frontier wars, as well as the so-called National Suicide of the Xhosa in 1856-57. He is wrapped in a floor-length leopard-skin mantle and, like the Dutch king, holds a staff, as well as a spear. The Khoi queen is similarly clad in a fringed leopard mantle. The king and queen wear earrings and necklaces created from shells and animal teeth. Both wear leather loincloths.

Nguni • Pawn

The Dutch rook/castle represents the original Dutch Fort de Goede Hoop of 1652, designed from details on 17th century maps, and from the 1686 French edition of Dapper, source for the front elevation. The base sections of all Dutch pieces are from a simplified outline of the fort structure. The Khoi rook/castle is shaped like a kraal, based on depictions by Abraham Bogaert, 1711, and Peter Kolb, 1719. The base sections of all Khoi pieces are a simplified version of one of the huts in the kraal, constructed from saplings and covered in woven reed mats.

The Dutch bishop is dressed in a square cap, ruff, rochet and chimere—the clerical dress rejected by the Puritans. This was taken from a woodcut of the 16th/17th century. The Khoi bishop is the indigenous 'sangoma,' the witch doctor drawn by F. T. I'Ons, from the William Fehr Collection.

The Dutch knight is in the usual horse-head shape. The Khoi knight, however, takes the form of the extinct *quagga*, the last one of which apparently died in 1883 in the Amsterdam zoo.

The Dutch pawns are arquebusiers [early musketeers], with military buffcoats over doublets, wearing breeches of the day, caught at the knee. Their metal helmets or *morions* are plumed and have small rims and ridges across the crown from front to back. They wear shoulder belts or 'collars of bandoliers' filled with gunpowder. Their weapons are the muskets in general use at the time. The Khoi pawns are based on an illustration by Georg Meister, dated 1688. They wear fur capes, and loincloths with feather, shell and leather accessories. The bows, arrows and quiver bags are from an illustration by Sparman in 1783.

SOUTH AFRICA
NGUNI
Figure 40 • Composition

Nguni is a broad ethnic category encompassing a number of peoples and language groups, including the Zulu and Xhosa. Nelson Mandela is a Xhosa. The other large language group in southern Africa is the Sotho. The Nguni and Sotho languages are as distinct from each other as the Germanic and Romance.

The attractiveness of this chess set derives largely from its representation of different ethnic groups, including Tsonga, Zulu, and Pondo. The Tsonga, who were conquered by Nguni-speaking people before the arrival of the Europeans, live well to the north of the Xhosa. Although there is a small Xhosa tribe, the general term "Xhosa," as used in South Africa, covers a broad grouping that includes the Tembu and Pondo.

The red Pawns are Tsonga women shown drinking from beer pots. The custom of fermenting maize to make beer is common. The blue Pawns represent married Pondo women wearing white, the symbol of goodness, and carrying fowls to be used in a sacrifice.

The Bishop is an elaborate Zulu sangoma. The small, round, brown balls on the Bishop's head represent the inflated bladders of sacrificial goats worn by sangomas.

The Castles are modeled on Xhosa huts (*rontawuli*) that have clay walls; thatch roofs; and floors made of clay and cow dung mixed together, smeared by hand, and polished into a hard, shiny-clean surface. I've eaten many a meal in such huts.

The King wears the royal leopard skins. The Knight is the rare mountain zebra which has been protected since 1937 in the National Park of Cape Province.

SOUTH AFRICA
ZULU

Figure 41 and Cover • Ivory

My association with Zulus is long and varied. It began with my first trip to Zululand, a kingdom in the Natal Province of South Africa, in 1949.

It continued in London a few years later when, while browsing through the third basement of a Soho shop that had been blitzed by the Germans, I found what is believed to be the only signature by the otherwise illiterate Zulu king Cetewayo.

Cetewayo roundly defeated the British at the famous battle of Isandhlwana on January 22, 1879. His soldiers killed Prince Imperial Louis Napoleon IV who, historians speculate, might well have become King of France. Prime Minster Disraeli is said to have commented, "A very remarkable people, the Zulus. They defeat our generals; they convert our bishops; they have settled the fate of a great European dynasty."

On August 28, 1879, Cetewayo was captured by the British after losing the Battle of Ulundi. He was taken by ship from Durban to Cape Town. While gazing over the magnificent view of Table Bay and the mountain from his quarters in the five-sided castle, he reportedly said, "I am a very old man." He was fifty-four. Later he was restored as ruler of part of his kingdom. But again he went into battle and was defeated by the British at Eshowe where he died in February 1884.

What I found in the London shop in 1949 was a handwritten letter by Mary Frere, daughter of Sir Bartle Frere who had become governor of the Cape of Good Hope in 1877, to her Uncle George in England. In the letter Mary described how she had taught Cetewayo to print his name in block letters. Above his signature she wrote: "Here is his name written by himself!"[12]

On different occasions in the 1970s, when Chief Mangosuthu Buthelezi and King Goodwill of Zululand saw the rare document in my office at Caltech, they wept. Eventually, I will give the letter with its famous signature to the Zulu or South African archives.

Zulu • Knight

A very different connection with the Zulus revolved around my efforts to help Chief Buthelezi's daughter Xolo with her college career in 1980. At the time, Buthelezi was Chancellor of the University of Zululand. Nineteen-year-old Xolo was a student there, although not a very good one. In part the problem may have been because the hostility of most of the Zulu students towards her father extended to her.

Dislike of the monarchy is widespread among the students. Most of them support the African National Congress (ANC) rather than Buthelezi's Inkatha

Party. Buthelezi's supporters are, in general, rural and uneducated.

On one occasion Buthelezi was rudely received by students who taunted his loyal bodyguards about their ignorance and tribal ways. The *impis*, a traditional Zulu battle unit, attacked the students, killing several and injuring many. Not a happy environment for Xolo.

So, through the intervention of friends, including me, Xolo was enrolled as a student at Pitzer College in Claremont, California where she roomed with four other women. She was under instructions not to answer the telephone herself because, she said, she had received threats from the ANC.

Although she was a lovely young woman, she was not enthusiastic about studying, even in California. She preferred to go shopping with a wealthy friend. On one such spree the friend bought expensive clothes. Although Xolo had been brought up in the corridors of power, she was without money herself. But she apparently could not resist some costly silk blouses. She was caught by the store's security guard and faced formal charges.

I was called to help her through the embarrassing situation. Her father was sympathetic. He asked me to thwart any publicity and to find a lawyer who would assist Xolo pro bono. An attorney friend who had been a high school exchange student in Port Elizabeth agreed to take on the pro bono assignment. Xolo was placed on probation and assigned to perform community service. I picked her up at 5:00 one morning and put her on a plane to South Africa.

But she came back to Pitzer, studied more diligently, and improved her grades. All went well until she was arrested again. She phoned me at 2:00 A.M. with a charming story. A woman friend who had

herpes also had a hot date. Not wanting to pass on the disease, the friend asked Xolo if she would go to the drugstore to pick up some condoms. Xolo obliged. She also picked up some lipstick and bracelets which she "forgot" to pay for. I received a rash of phone calls from her father, the South African ambassador, the Department of State. Again Xolo was defended pro bono by the generous lawyer. The result: she was found guilty. But she left the country before sentencing.

She is now in Ulundi, Zululand and has a child. I have advised her not to request a visa and, if granted one, not to come to the United States again.

My most memorable Zulu experience was of an entirely different nature: a visit with Chief Albert John Luthuli in 1953 after he was elected president of the African National Congress. Luthuli was a noble man, literate, cultured, and principled; a man of vigor and action. His last name means dust. Perhaps it referred to the dust that swirled behind him when he was in full stride.

I had heard him address a meeting of all races in Cape Town and was deeply impressed with his Lincolnian qualities of integrity and vision.

Afterwards, on May 6, 1953, I drove to his home. The tarred north coast road out of Durban wound between rounded hills carpeted with sugar cane. Single-lane, steel bridges crossed dry riverbeds. Knots of Hindu factory workers, well-dressed descendants of their indentured forefathers, stood outside Gandhi Cinema. A car loaded with shouting, European teenagers careered past a young Zulu who was relieving himself by the roadside. I passed the site of one of Shaka's royal kraals (an enclosure of huts). Across the hills smoke rose from burning cane, a simulation of another day more than a century earlier when Shaka's impis raided and burned the kraal of a recalcitrant chief.

Across the Etete River and down a winding lane that dwindled into a sandy track, I found Luthuli's homestead—a farm of forty acres, ten owned, the rest leased.

Although his small bungalow was the most substantial Zulu home in the area, it was not impressive by Western standards. In front of the house a barefoot old woman, whom I later learned was Luthuli's aunt, was drying rice by sifting it in the sun. She greeted me in Zulu and called through the front door to Luthuli.

After a few formal minutes in the living room we moved outside to the stoep, a simple porch. It was a warm autumn afternoon. We took off our coats and settled back in comfortable chairs for a long talk that covered many topics.

I learned that, in 1935, when Luthuli was teaching languages and Zulu music and supervising practice teachers at Adams College in Natal, he was called home to serve his people as district chief. The area had been designated a special mission reserve many years before and had long had democratically elected chiefs. More than eighty years before, Luthuli's grandfather had been elected to that office.

Luthuli said he was surprised to be elected president of the ANC. There had been no rumor of support for him, although he had been leader of the Natal Province branch of the ANC.

In his capacity as chief, Luthuli had been called to Pretoria by the government to persuade him to give up leadership of the Passive Defiance movement against the country's laws. He explained, "After coming back here and thinking it over, I felt

they were justified in feeling I couldn't serve two causes, so I resigned as chief. Although my position was untenable from their viewpoint, I was truly leading my people in both capacities." His successor as chief was a close friend whom Luthuli called his "trouble messenger."

Luthuli believed the Passive Defiance movement absolutely depended on the participation of women, who outnumbered men in most of the Defiance groups.

He told me emphatically that the general African attitude toward Europeans contained an enormous amount of goodwill, particularly in regard to the churches. He repeatedly praised the missionaries, including American ones in his own district, for what they had brought to the African people.

He opposed nationalism as a permanent force because, as he explained, "We must not have Africans voting for Africans someday without considering relative ability. The nationalism of the Afrikaners is a terrible example for *our* nationalism."

As we continued to talk, a pretty young woman came out to the stoep with tea and cake. Miss Mdhuli was Luthuli's cousin and a teacher in the local school. She asked about the United States. Luthuli recalled how well he had been treated on his visit there and expressed admiration for the spiritual and material sides of America.

The afternoon ended with a rapidly setting sun. A young man walked by strumming a guitar. Just beyond the front yard a small boy, no more than five or six years old, drove a herd of some thirty long-horned cattle back to their kraal. It was time for me to leave.

For several months after my visit with Luthuli, he was under close watch by the police. They even

Ndebele • Bishop

Zulu • Bishop

watched me. Two months after my visit he was banned from any public gathering. But seven years later, when he was awarded the Nobel Peace Prize, he was permitted to go to Oslo to receive it. He then wrote his autobiography, *Let My People Go*.[13]

In 1967 he was killed by a train while crossing a trestle within walking distance of the stoep where we had talked. Just writing these words brings tears to my eyes.

Many lives, both black and white, would have been saved if Luthuli's message had been heard by the government of South Africa. Unfortunately, at the time, the National Party did not have a leader of equal vision to work with him in the kind of effort that Mandela and De Klerk were to make three decades later.

The magnificent set pictured here was carved in 1979 by Mr. B. J. Shozi of Inanda in Natal Province. The ivory was stained with tea to make the black side.

Unfortunately, Mr. Shozi has been unable to carve for a number of years because he suffered severe hand injuries in a bus accident. Despite rehabilitation efforts, the prognosis is not good.

When I showed the set to members of the Anthropology Department at the University of Witwatersrand and to Pierre Jacques, a long-time medical missionary who has worked among the Shangaan people in Mozambique, I was told that it is an anthropologically correct representation of Zulu culture, with some exceptions.

The consensus was that the Queen's headdress is more Pondomisse (a sub-group of the Xhosa who belong, like the Zulus, to the broad Nguni language group) than Zulu. The double-story granary for the Castle is more suggestive of the Shangaan.

Ndebele • King

SOUTH AFRICA
NDEBELE VS. ZULU
Figures 42a and 42b • Composition and Wood

The Ndebele, one of the more peaceful groups of Sotho-speaking peoples, are represented on the white side, with bases made of jacaranda wood. The Ndebele are best known for the geometric designs with which they adorn their huts. The Knight is a giraffe, common in the grasslands of the north where the Ndebele reside.

The dark side, with bases made of teakwood (*kiaathout* in Afrikaans), represents the Zulu, the most famous warrior nation in southern Africa. The Zulus were usually the aggressors against the Sotho peoples in what are now the northern provinces of South Africa. Thus, the Zulu Pawns carry fighting shields, which are decorated to resemble buffalo hide. The Knight is a zebra. Just as the Zulu King is taller than the Ndebele King, the Zulu Queen is taller than her Ndebele counterpart.

Laura Gerhart, the artist of this set, lives in Parys in the Free State, formerly called the Orange Free State. The Mandela government dropped the "Orange."

SOUTH AFRICA
NDEBELE
Figure 43 • Clay

Half of the black African peoples of South Africa are Sotho-speaking. The Sotho are generally less hierarchical than the other major southern African grouping, the Nguni peoples.

Among the Sotho, the Ndebele are known for their colorful decorations and distinctive designs. They also excel in beadwork, and their aprons can be works of art. In the chess set, the Queen's apron of red, yellow, blue, and white is illustrative of the Ndebele's colorful dress.

Joshua Ngenya, the artist who made this set while living near Rustenburg in the western Transvaal, has exhibited his sculpture in Johannesburg galleries.

SOUTH AFRICA
TOWNSHIP ART

Figure 44 • Wire

"Township" is the generic word for African suburbs. Soweto is an acronym for South Western Townships of Johannesburg, as contrasted with Alexandria, a township on the northern fringe of Johannesburg. Alexandria is now being incorporated with Sandton, a formerly all-white area.

Township art is not to be ignored in a collection such as this because it is rooted in the community, and it often reflects great ingenuity and talent.

Copper wire is the main material used to create township art, although all kinds of wire—even the more valuable, plated type—may be used. Whether the wire comes directly from wholesalers is questionable, but no one has yet made a direct connection between a disconnected telephone line and an art product on a shopping mall sidewalk. Wire toys of all sorts abound. Some are wonderfully mobile. Wire motorcycles can be up to ten feet long, and are frequently purchased for young white boys with easily persuaded parents.

This particular chess set grew out of a conversation with a group of young men, most of them from Zimbabwe, who congregate in a shopping mall in the fashionable part of suburban Rosebank. Under the direction of one member of the group, Steve Chizero, they assembled the entire set over a long weekend.

What a contrast to another experience. A friend had contacted a talented wire toy-maker in the Cape Town suburb of Montagu about making a set for me. When the artisan was told the set was for an American

collector, he drove my friend to distraction with worry about adhering to "political correctness." The debate dragged on for three years, and I never got the set.

So you can imagine my surprise in having the Rosebank set created in one weekend. Next time I'm there I'll look to see whether it has been duplicated. Street vendors are keenly attuned to the marketplace; what sells is usually quickly replicated.

Township • Castle

Township art is a distinct genre and should be respected as such. Unfortunately, some tourists and white South Africans assume it is *the* art of Africa, not realizing that there are black South African artists whose talents are recognized worldwide.

An example of such ignorance occurred several years ago at a party in my Pasadena home. One of the guests was my late friend Sydney Kumalo, an internationally acclaimed sculptor who had exhibited at the Venice and Sao Paulo Biennials. His massive bronzes cost upwards of $50,000 just to cast. He owned a lavish, two-story home in Dube. He came to the party dressed informally, in a leather jacket and jeans. Another guest, a famous art collector who was unaware of Kumalo's achievements, spoke patronizingly to him and condescendingly about black art from South Africa.[14]

SOUTH AFRICA
ANIMALS

Figure 45 • Ivory

This set could well be described as generic African. The lion is King; the lioness, Queen. There may be intended irony in portraying the Bishop as a vulture. The Knight is a warthog. A hippo makes an impressive Castle. For some indiscernible reason, the largest African animal, the elephant, represents the smallest chess piece, the Pawn.

King

SOUTH AFRICA
SOTHO, XHOSA, PONDO & ZULU
Figures 46a, b, c, d • Porcelain

Sotho • Queen

Elsa van Laere lives in the small eastern Cape town of Addo, about an hour's drive north of Port Elizabeth, the industrial center. Addo lies in the Suurberg Mountains (*suur* means sour or acid in Afrikaans) and is famed as the home of a small band of elephants, survivors of a larger number that once dominated the evergreen shrub countryside.

Although I have never met Van Laere, we have often chatted on the telephone. She is Afrikaans and speaks with a broad accent. Our conversations are sprinkled with Afrikaans expressions.

Early in her career, she was a medical technician. Then, in Addo, she was a farmer. She built a reservoir on the farm; bred Dexter cattle, performing the artificial insemination herself; and even bred bulldogs.

About ten years ago an accident forced her to give up farming. Seeking a new source of income, she turned to pottery. She processes and markets terra cotta and produces a wide range of craft goods.

Van Laere has meticulously copied the artistic styles of the major South African ethnic groups. For many years her exquisite, individual figurines—such as a Xhosa woman smoking a pipe, reminiscent of many such women I have seen in the Transkei—were sold in pricey gift shops. Her work became widely known under the rubric "Elsa's Little People." She has produced figures from twelve different African groups in the Republic of South Africa.

--- ••• ---

In time she began to produce chess sets, usually depicting one ethnic group against another, such as Zulu versus their close cousins and strong rivals the Xhosa.

Swaziland • Queen

The major pieces in each set are authentic and thus different, although she does use the same cow mold for more than one set and has duplicated straw huts as Castles. However, her Xhosa Castle hut is distinctly different from the Castle hut of the Pondo subgroup of the Xhosa. Some of her Pawns are similar.

From the authenticity of her figures, one might expect that she had deep insight into African cultures resulting from long study. In fact, she has surprisingly little knowledge of the subject outside of what she needs to know to create the figures. Yet I have never heard Africans or others who should know, such as anthropologists, question her details of dress. Her attention to detail means that each piece goes through three paintings and three firings. And each piece is signed and numbered.

Van Laere is not sympathetic to recent political developments in the eastern Cape. She would have sold her farm and moved to Cape Town if farm prices had not tumbled to abysmal levels and remained there for some time. She does not expect her children to remain on the farm and seeks the relative safety of Cape Town for them.

Elsa van Laere is an exceptionally talented and determined woman who has produced, and I hope will continue to produce, some of the most delightful and attractive chess sets in Africa.[15]

SWAZILAND
Figure 47 • Porcelain

With her characteristic attention to detail, Elsa van Laere has made the major Swazi pieces significantly different from those in her other sets. The King has a decorated buffalo shield, spear, and flounces around his ankles. The Queen has a decorated band around her headgear and necklace. Like the King, the Bishop, a sangoma, has long hair and wears a skullcap. He carries a magical fly whisk to suggest his occult powers.

SWAZILAND

Figure 48 and Cover • Green and Black Stone

Sishyi Nxumalo, who later became a cabinet minister, had just returned to Swaziland after completing his Ph.D. in the U.K. It was 1954 and we met while I was visiting his country to write an article about it.

The initial syllables of his first and last names are pronounced with a tongue click. In Swazi, "Sishyi" means, in effect, "I defeated you." It seems that, although Sishyi's father had forty-two wives, he fancied another young girl from a well-known family. But the girl's father adamantly refused to give his consent to the marriage. The suitor kidnapped the young beauty and, after consummating the union that resulted in my friend's birth, received her father's acquiescence. Hence Sishyi's apt name.

Thanks to his kind invitation I was a guest at his country's Independence Day in 1968. What a tumultuous weekend. There was incessant drumming for bare-breasted dancing girls. There were continuous parties and diplomatic receptions.

When I visited Swaziland again later, to speak at the fourth Libertarian International Congress, I was struck by the immense changes that had taken place. As an academic correspondent for the American Universities Field Staff, I had interviewed King Sobhuza on two trips to his country when it was still a British territory. Both times he was barefoot and wore the royal leopard skin. (He took it as a good omen that I was born in the year he became king: 1921.) Now he was the ruler of an independent nation that was

host to an international congress.

After King Sobhuza's death, Sishyi got trapped in tribal politics and spent a terrible year in prison in the early 1970s. I wrote to the Swazi Minister of Justice on Sishyi's behalf, asking for clemency and decent treatment in prison. Sishyi later told me that the minister had been influenced by the letters from his overseas supporters, and that their attention to his plight may have saved his life.

Swaziland • Queen

In this set the sides are distinguished only by color. I prefer sets that have the two sides in opposition, but the Swazis are such a peaceful people that they could not be arrayed against anyone—not Voortrekkers, Portuguese, or Zulus. As Sishyi's daughter Qondile told me, "When the Zulus came to fight us in the last century the Swazis surrendered immediately and made love, not war."

A subsequent unhappy result of Swazi pacifism was that they allowed fifty-four percent of their country to be taken by the whites. The Swazis are trying to reverse this situation now by restricting foreign (white) purchase of land outside the urban areas.

SWAZILAND

Figure 49 and Cover • Pewter

During a dinner with Sishyi in his country in 1989, I talked about my search for chess sets. He suggested that I contact McDonald Mashego, a Swazi and the first black pewtersmith in southern Africa. There were Malay pewtersmiths in Cape Town after the Dutch brought artisans from Java, but no black Africans.

Swazi live on both sides of the Swaziland-South African border. Mashego, who has only an eighth-grade education, lives in the small town of Pilgrim's

Pawn

Rest in the eastern Transvaal. He was trained in his craft by a German metallurgist brought to South Africa by the Scientific Council. Mashego showed me some of his molds and promised to let me have the first completed set, which he did. The pieces show traditional Swazi dress.

Although Mashego envisioned making fifty sets, and I anticipated seeing them in the better quality gift shops in southern Africa, I am aware of only two or three made after mine. I saw none on my most recent visits.

LESOTHO
MOSHOESHOE I
Figure 50 • Silver

King

The silver and sulphur-oxidized silver set weighs 800 grams (about 28.5 ounces). The design, made in Lesotho in 1983 by a German, Erhard Nolte, was originally cast in copper, but has been made only in silver since 1989. Most of the pieces are cast whole, but individual accoutrements are handmade and joined to the pieces with silver solder. About fifteen silver sets exist.

The King is Moshoeshoe I, one of the country's heroes, who lived from about 1790 to 1870. The Bishop is Moshoeshoe's spiritual advisor, Mohlomi. The Bishop's shield, with its wild animal skins topped by a magnificent ostrich feather, is based on the one Mohlomi wore.

In 1975 Nolte had adapted Mohlomi's shield, with the addition of the St. Andrew's cross (X), for the Scots' St. Andrew's Society of Basutoland, now known as Lesotho. The cross dates from about the eighth century and has been associated with St. Andrew, the patron saint of the Scots, since about the thirteenth century. The St. Andrew's cross has also

adorned the British flag, the Union Jack, since about 1606. When Nolte designed the chess set, he retained the cross on the Bishop's shield.

The Pawns' shields are those of an ordinary sangoma. The Castles are huts depicting typical Basotho design, with markings that are not specific to any clan.

I bought the set in 1992 at a small handicraft workshop on a potholed dirt street named after Mohlomi, in Maseru, the capital of Lesotho. I locked the set in the trunk of my rented car and went into a restaurant for lunch. When I came out, the set was gone. I had inadvertently left the driver's side window open just a fraction—enough for someone to slip a wire inside, open the door, and release the trunk latch.

Later, a number of people in Maseru told me they were not surprised at the theft. A Mosotho friend told me there were groups of children who purloined articles from cars in the parking lot, with a spy keeping an eye on the car owners inside the restaurant. Several people told me I was lucky; a few days previously a British couple in a Mercedes had been hijacked to the countryside, beaten, and robbed of their car.

I was able to return to the workshop and order another silver set from the same molds. Of course I had to pay for it again. More good luck, I guess.

The purpose of this visit to Lesotho, my fifth since 1950, was twofold: to look for chess sets, of course; and to observe at a workshop for women lawyers funded as part of a U.S. grant for human rights in Lesotho. Speaking at that workshop, Dr. Leonard Spearman, the American ambassador, said that a shift from military government to a constitutional framework would be the first step to transforming a legal system that discriminates against women.

Only two percent of the administrative posts in the country are held by women. In general, the women of Lesotho have a hard life. They perform the essential tasks that keep the country going: farming, teaching, shop keeping, and child-raising. Of course life is not easy for the men either. More than sixty percent of Basotho men work in the South African gold, coal, and platinum mines. The Basotho men who live in Lesotho work mainly in the civil service. Twenty-one percent are unemployed. Still, I heard a good many women who want a change toward equality of opportunity.

The most highly placed woman in recent years was the Lesotho Ambassador to Washington who lost her post after King Moshoeshoe II was overthrown in 1970. She is now the librarian of the University in Roma, a city in Lesotho. Her lovely, large library building is the result of a decade of largesse to Lesotho by major foreign donors who were looking for a way to justify remaining in South Africa. When I visited her there I found her to be a woman of immense energy and faith; but she confessed to being hard pressed by the shortage of money for books and journals.[16]

Some of the problems faced by professional, African American women are analogous to those of their counterparts in Lesotho. For example, divorced and single women in Lesotho often choose to have children outside of marriage. An administrator, a woman in her mid-thirties who drove me from the university campus in Roma to my hotel in Maseru, explained it bluntly: "There are no men for a woman like me to marry. But I wanted children and I'm glad that I have two. We often discuss this because almost all of my [female] friends are unmarried but have children."

TRISTAN DA CUNHA

Figure 51 • Wood, Postage Stamps, and Painted Designs

Tristan • King

There is no airfield on Tristan da Cunha. Union Castle passenger liners used to make occasional stops on their fourteen-day run from Southampton to Cape Town. Twice I stood off the island without being able to land due to bad weather. One way to get there nowadays is on the mail and supply ship that calls only once each year. Perhaps that is why a book and television documentary about Tristan called it *The Loneliest Island in the World.*[17]

But that description is hyperbole. In fact, weather permitting, one or two private yachts manage to land every year; the odd cruise ship calls; and there are the fishing boats that carry Tristan's lobster catch to the Cape Town market.

On a lonely island where, in the past, years might pass without a ship calling, great occasions are appropriately celebrated by the issuing of postage stamps. Equally appropriate is the predominance of stamps on this chess set—which, as far as I know, is the first one from Tristan. It was designed by Ian Lavarello, a Tristaner who wrote that the carving was done by a Mr. R. Glass and the painting by a "deaf and dumb lad," Mr. J. Rogers. Lavarello explained that there was not time to have pictures painted on all the pieces because the mail ship arrived unexpectedly early.

The major figures on the black side are distinguished both by shape and stamps. On the Castles are stamps commemorating the fiftieth anniversary of the end of World War II. Stamps on the Bishops depict the 1935 visit of the liner *Empress of Australia*. The Pawns feature a one pence stamp showing the *Duchess of Atholl*, which visited Tristan in 1929, and a five pence stamp of the *Anatolia*, which visited in 1937.

Major white pieces depict various aspects of island life, including a spinning wheel and uninhabited Nightingale Island, where intrepid young men occasionally go for provisions. Fittingly, the King shows the volcano that dominates the island. The Queen is illustrated by a painting of the nearby, almost-never-visited island named Inaccessible. Could there be some Freudian significance in associating the Queen with that island?

Paintings on the white Pawns show more vignettes of island life and include penguins, lobsters or crayfish, gulls, a flying falcon, a seal, fishing and sailing boats, and a beach.

My successful effort to obtain a Tristan chess set in 1995 took a somewhat circuitous route. It meant catching a ship, the *Hanseatic*, in Ushuaia (the southernmost city in the world, at the tip of Argentina); spending two weeks in the Antarctic stopping at various sub-Antarctic islands, such as South Georgia, where Ernest Shackleton is buried; and then steaming ahead four days from the roaring forties to Tristan. The *Hanseatic* had run into such heavy seas the previous year that she had abandoned her scheduled stop at Tristan. So you know that I kept an anxious eye on the weather forecasts and barometer as we approached the island.

Luckily the seas were reasonably calm. When the *Hanseatic* anchored I made sure to be in the first rubber Zodiac to land at the small concrete quay in barely sheltered Edinburgh.

Tristan was settled when the British established a small contingent there to help guard against a French rescue of Napoleon from St. Helena, about five hundred miles to the north.[18]

When the British left the island, one of the soldiers was allowed to stay. From time to time there were shipwrecks or emergency landings and a sailor or two would opt to remain. The population grew, but has never exceeded more than about three hundred.

In 1961 the volcano that dominates Tristan erupted. The terrified islanders took temporary refuge on nearby uninhabited Nightingale Island. Later many of them settled on an abandoned air force base in England; some moved to Cape Town. Eventually most returned to their crime-free island home. The community now is made up of just a few families, mostly of English and Italian origin.

Some Tristaners, who came from St. Helena but were originally from the Coloured community of Cape Town, have brown complexions. However, there appear to be no color distinctions drawn on the island.

Thanks to the wonderful hospitality of the Tristaners, I was able to enjoy many informative conversations as I walked the paved and unpaved narrow streets of Edinburgh. The town resembles an English village. The homes have neat fences, names at the gates, and a profusion of subtropical and middle-latitude flowers. Before the volcano erupted, with lava flowing down to the edge of the village and creating new land in the sea, the single story cottages had thatched roofs. Now, based on what the refugees learned during their stay in England, the cottages are roofed with galvanized iron. Unfortunately, the benefit of better protection from the rain and less maintenance has a considerable aesthetic cost.

My visit to the forty-square-mile island coincided with potato day—the one day each week that every inhabitant is supposed to walk a few miles to the potato patch and hoe. Most were finished and back in their cottages by early afternoon. There is also an apple orchard in one corner of the island.

Money comes from the sale of lobsters caught with pots hauled up from open boats unique to the island. Money also comes from knitted goods. Lambs abound, supplying beautiful wool that is homespun.

With a stretch of imagination, you could say Tristan has a golf course. The governor arranged a round on the nine holes, which the *Hanseatic*'s captain wanted to play. The captain and I both got navy blue ties with "TCCC" initialed in white—Tristan da Cunha Country Club. ▦

NOTES

PREFACE

1. Paul Gottlieb, president of Abrams, an art book publisher in the U.S., expressed strong interest in this book; however, he wanted it to be a history of chess sets. I simply don't have the knowledge—or the decades it would take to acquire the knowledge—to even essay a book on chess set history.

2. While at the Presidio, I moonlighted to help build a new cannery for pilchards, made famous in Steinbeck's *Cannery Row*. By the time we finished the factory the pilchards had mysteriously departed, and the cannery never processed a single fish. The converted cannery is now a restaurant, with lots of fish on the menu.

3. After the war Schmidt returned to his family in Leipzig—including a daughter who had been born during his service in North Africa where he had been captured. We kept in touch with him and each Christmas sent toys and a larger-sized outfit for his daughter. In return we received successive photographs of the girl growing into her teens. Then, unexpectedly, came a sad letter begging us not to send anything else; in the rising tensions created by the Cold War, the Schmidts were under suspicion because they received packages from America. From time to time I have tried to contact the family, to no avail. Even with the end of the Cold War and the demolishing of the Berlin Wall, I doubt that I will ever find the now middle-aged daughter whose father started my chess collection.

INTRODUCTION TO THE SERIES

1. One such book is H. J. R. Murray's monumental *History of Chess* (Oxford: Clarendon Press, 1913).

2. Izak Linder, *The Art of Chess Pieces* (Moscow: H.G.S. 1994).

3. The first American writing on chess was Benjamin Franklin's "The Morals of Chess," published in *The Columbian Magazine* in December 1786.

4. Thomas Henry Huxley, *A Liberal Education* (1868).

INTRODUCTION TO VOLUME 1

1. The annual arrivals of the Omani ships were first written about in 1 A.D. in *Periplus Maris Erythraei*; the Greek description of the East African coast includes Zanzibar and the neighboring island of Pemba.

2. Randall Pouwels, *Horn and the Crescent* (Cambridge: University Press, 1987).

3. See note 1 in Introduction to the Series, above (p.364).

4. W. C. Plowden, *Travels in Abyssinia* (London: Longman, Greens & Co., 1868).

5. O. G. S. Crawford, *Ethiopian Itineraries, Circa 1400-1524* (Cambridge: 1955). Among the many references to Ethiopian chess sets are those by Richard Pankhurst: *A Social History of Ethiopia* (Trenton, NJ: The Red Sea Press, 1992); "History and Principles of Ethiopian Chess," *Santaraj Journal of Ethiopian Studies*, Vol. 9, Number 2, 1971, pp.149-170; "Ethiopian Chess: A Game of Yesteryear," *The British Chess Magazine*, Vol. 105, 1985, pp. 287-290. His work is well researched and detailed.

6. In the summer of 1995 the avid British collector Vel Williams saw the British Museum's Bornu set on display at the Hastings Museum, which was celebrating the one hundredth anniversary of tournament chess in Hastings. Williams said that, unfortunately, a number of the main pieces were cracked, and the small pieces of cloth used to distinguish the Mai from the Chiroma were missing on both sides. The curator apparently was not aware that the cloth was missing nor of its importance.

7. There is another Bornu set owned by Guy Betts, a farmer near Oxford. Betts worked in Maiduguri, Bornu and Jos, Nigeria many years ago. The curator of the Pitt-Rivers Museum at Oxford, Bernard Fagg, has been trying since 1969 to convince Betts to bequeath the set to the museum. Betts's set differs from the others in one regard: one side is slightly charred to make it black. According to Betts, who played the game (tsatsarandi),

the King, Castle, and Knight move as in modern chess. The Bishop can use only four squares, but if the next one is occupied, it can jump like a Knight. The Queen can use only the four adjacent diagonal squares. Pawns cannot be promoted when reaching the eighth rank, and there is no castling. It follows that the Castle is the strongest piece on the board and justifies its name: kaigama or commander-in-chief.

8. The photograph also shows the Pawns as *gollo;* the Knight, a horse; the Bishop, a court official (*bintu*); and the Queen, heir apparent (*chiroma*). The King represents *mai,* as the ancient kings of Bornu were called. The King differs from the Queen only by having a small white cloth.

9. Sir Richard Palmer, *The Bornu Sahara and Sudan* (London: John Murray, 1936).

10. Jessie McNab, *Chess: East and West, Past and Present* (New York: Harry Abrams, 1968).

11. This theme is picked up in my 1995 novella *Rwanda,* available at the Caltech bookstore.

12. Ekpo Eyo, *Primitivism and Other Misconceptions in African Art* (Munger Africana Library Notes, April 1982, Volume 63). Eyo reiterated his beliefs in his address to my African seminar at Caltech.

    Over a period of fifteen years I published seventy-five issues of Munger Africana Library Notes through the California Institute of Technology. As a publisher I was able to break academic restraints and frequently did so. For example, I printed the first detailed account of female circumcision, fifteen years before Alice Walker made its horrifying details the centerpiece of a best-selling novel. That article, along with Orson Welles's account of Karen Blixen, aka Isak Dinesen, and Regusters's strange story of an extant dinosaur, brought the most inquiries—from every corner of the world.

13. *The Kano Chronicle* has been edited and translated by R. Palmer. It can be found in Palmer's *Sudanese Memoirs* (Lagos, Nigeria: Government Printer, 1928).

PART 1: EASTERN AFRICA

1. Edwin S. Munger, *Relational Patterns of Kampala, Uganda* (Chicago: University of Chicago Press, 1951).

2. This is analogous to the position of the Zulu kingdom within South Africa.

3. Reverend Sams had the vision and courage to establish the Christian University of East Africa, the only private university in Africa south of Egypt. With his own savings, acquired during his employment as an Episcopal priest in Southern California, he purchased from me a large number of Uganda books and journals at a fraction of their auction price.

4. Kalema accompanied King Mutebi to California in June 1994. Twenty years earlier, Kalema was the brightest science student produced by the crack Budo secondary school. However, he had not done well in the Cambridge exams. Just before the exams he had flown home to Buganda to attend the funeral of his father, who had been murdered by General Amin. Subsequently Kalema got an inferior position as an engineer in a Zambia copper mine. At the urging of my friend Dr. Martin Aliker, I succeeded in getting Kalema admitted to Caltech. Finding money for his tuition and living costs was a struggle. Thus it was with great pride that I saw him receive his Ph.D. in chemical engineering. He worked for Du Pont for several years before returning to Buganda.

5. Dr. Philip Githinji was the first Kikuyu to pursue graduate studies at my university and the first black chosen for the Distinguished Alumni Award by Caltech. He became vice chancellor of Kenyatta University, the second university in Kenya.

6. This detailed information on Malawi sets comes through the kindness of a dear friend, Donald Brody, the Consul General of Malawi in Seattle and a confidant of former President Banda.

7. Brody emphatically disagrees with me.

PART 2: WESTERN AFRICA

1. Werner Muensterberger, *Collecting: An Unruly Passion* (Princeton University Press: Princeton, 1993).

2. Adam Phillips, the *New York Times* (December 12, 1993).

3. Hans and Siegfried Wichmann, *Shach* (Callwey: Munich, 1960). Their book is dedicated to Maunoury, who wrote the foreword.

4. Victor Keats, CHESSMEN *for Collectors* (London: Batsford, 1985).

5. Filomina Chioma Steady's study of Sierra Leone politics, "Female Power in African Politics: The National Congress of Sierra Leone," appears in *Munger Africana Library Notes*, Vol. 6, (1975) Issue 31.

6. See note 4 above.

7. Another example of stereotyping is evident in the photograph of a different African set in the April 3, 1980 Christies catalog: one of the pieces is a melon. As all Americans know, African Americans have long had an antipathy to the depiction of blacks eating watermelon.

8. According to Franz Josef Lang, the prominent German collector and expert on markings, the 1995 price is $2,200. Add $500 if you want it with an accompanying board, which looks like a big plate.

9. George Chèvres, "Christians in Chad: Responding to God, Responding to War" (*Munger Africana Library Notes*, December, 1983, Issue 71).

PART 3: CENTRAL AFRICA

1. Herman Regusters, "Mokele-Mbembe: An Investigation into Rumors Concerning a Strange Animal in the Republic of the Congo" (*Munger Africana Library Notes*, Vol. 12, Issue 64, July 1982).

2. *Encyclopedia Britannica Atlas*, 1949-1961.

3. The Matabele, whose King Lobengula negotiated with Rhodes, are popularly known as warrior-cattle people. They are one of the offshoots of the Zulu expansion. The occasionally nomadic cattle people in Africa are usually not as strong in artistic expression as the more sedentary crop growers, such as the Shona. I have never seen a Matabele-inspired chess set.

4. Descargues' comment appeared in a review of 100 Shona sculptures exhibited at the Musee Rodin in 1971, as quoted by Anthony and Laura Ponter in *Spirits in Stone* (California: Ukama Press, 1992).

5. Credit for the development of Shona art must also be given to Malawian carvers who turn up all over eastern and southern Africa. Of the twenty-five original carvers encouraged by McEwen, approximately twenty were Malawians, according to my well-informed friend Donald Brody, who knows Malawai like the back of his hand. The work by the Malawians has a generic Shona style and is recognized as Shona.

6. Also quoted by the Ponters (see note 4 above).

7. See Ponter, p.28.

8. Basil Davidson has written more than twenty books on Africa, including *The Africa Slave Trade*, *The Lost Cities of Africa*, *No Fist Is Big Enough to Hide the Sky*, *The Story of Africa*, and *The Black Man's Burden: Africa and the Curse of the Nation-State*, named a Notable Book of the Year by *The New York Times* in 1992.

9. Frank Greygoose, *Chessman* (NY: Arco, 1967).

10. I first visited San settlements when studying Bechuanaland in the 1960s on a Rockefeller Brothers Foundation grant, and later wrote the first book on the country by an American—*Bechuanaland: Bantu Homeland or Pan African Outpost?* (London: Oxford University Press, 1967). I concluded that Bechuanaland would follow neither alternative offered in the title, and that has proven to be the case.

PART 4: SOUTHERN AFRICA

1. Alan Paton, *Cry, the Beloved Country* (New York: Charles Scribner's Sons, 1948).

2. M. C. Botha, "Blood Gene Frequencies as an Indication of the Genetic Constitution of Population Samples in Cape Town," *Munger Africana Library Notes*, Vol. 16, October 1972.

3. Abubakr Effendi, *Demonstration of the Religious Practice of Islam*, with an English translation by Mia Brandel-Syrier.

4. Alan Paton, *Too Late the Phalarope* (New York: Charles Scribner's Sons, 1953).

5. Paton stated his liberal views in a long article, "The Afrikaner as I Know Him," which appeared in a book I edited: *The Afrikaners* (Cape Town: Tafelberg, 1979).

6. Peter F. Alexander, *Alan Paton: A Biography* (London: Oxford University Press, 1994).

7. Alan Paton wrote several autobiographical works, all published by Charles Scribner's Sons, New York: *For You Departed* (1969); *Towards the Mountain: An Autobiography* (1980); and *Journey Continued* (1988).

8. It was Dick van der Ross who asked me to form the Cape of Good Hope Foundation, which has poured two million dollars into the University of the Western Cape and other largely Coloured and black institutions since 1986.

9. Gabeba Abrahams, "The Archaeological Potential of Central Cape Town," *Munger Africana Library Notes*, Issues 77/78, September 1985.

10. As a member of the scientific board of Earthwatch of Boston, Massachusetts, I was able to sponsor Gabeba Abrahams for a grant, which brought relays of volunteers to Cape Town to dig up the old parade ground. From time to time, the diggers stopped their excavations and called Abrahams to examine an archaeological find, often in the glare of television cameras.

11. A fund associated with the Leakey Foundation, the Baldwin Fund, for which I was trustee, has now trained almost thirty Africans from all over the continent to the Ph.D. level.

12. The aging spinster who ran the shop where I bought the letter was surprised by my find and hesitated before she accepted my modest offer for it. On my subsequent visits to the shop's new, plush quarters in Mayfair, she never failed to tell me how sorry she was that she had let the Cetewayo signature go. King Cetawayo's exploits are depicted in *Zulu*, a magnificent, three-and-one-half-hour British film. For American audiences the film is usually cut to a disjointed two hours.

13. Albert John Luthuli, *Let My People Go* (London: Collins, 1962).

14. Subsequently, in 1962, the now defunct South African magazine *News/Check* published my detailed account of the outrageous conversation.

15. Collectors can still reach Van Laere at Box 175, Addo 6105. Her chess sets obviously require much detailed and skilled hand labor. Out of economic necessity, she prices them high for sale in the finer hotel and gift shops. However, she will sell sets wholesale and without the expensive boxes that accompany sets sold to the carriage trade.

16. Since then the Cape of Good Hope Foundation has sent materials to the library of the University at Roma on a number of occasions.

17. N. and G. Humphries, *Tristan da Cunha: A Photoguide to the World's Loneliest Island in the South Atlantic Ocean* (London: Oxford, 1982).

18. David Hapgood, *The Murder of Napoleon* (New York: St. Martins Press, 1982). While researching his exciting book about Napoleon being poisoned on St. Helena, Hapgood learned that Napoleon had received a chess set there as a gift from India. It seems that the governor kept it for a while before allowing Napoleon to play with it.

INDEX

ABOUT THE AUTHOR

Ned Munger is an authority on the geography, history, and politics of sub-Saharan Africa. He is professor emeritus at the California Institute of Technology, where he taught African Studies for forty years. Much of his knowledge was gained first-hand during eighty-nine visits to the countries and islands of Africa. Many of those visits involved protracted periods of study, beginning with research for his master's thesis in Liberia and his doctoral dissertation in Uganda. He was the first Fulbright scholar to Africa and received a grant from the Rockefeller Brothers Foundation for three African study trips.

Dr. Munger has also traveled widely throughout the rest of the world, visiting more than 300 countries and islands in the Americas, Europe, Asia, Polynesia, Melanesia, Micronesia, the Far and Middle East, and Antarctica. Most of his early travels were as a Fellow of the Institute of Current World Affairs (Crane Rogers Foundation) and as a correspondent of the American Universities Field Staff.

Those travels fueled his passion for collecting chess sets that represent the cultures and countries he visited and studied.

For fourteen years Dr. Munger was president of the L. S. B. Leakey Foundation, which pioneered the study of early man in a three-pronged approach: archaeological fossils with the Leakeys, Johanson, and White; higher primates with Goodall, Fossey, and Galdikas; and hunter-gatherers with Devore and others.

Dr. Munger was a founder-trustee of the African Studies Association and the African-American Institute; launched the Baldwin Fellowships, which helped forty Africans obtain advanced degrees in archaeology; and, since 1985, has been president of the Cape of Good Hope Foundation, which has sent more than two million dollars worth of books to black universities in southern Africa. He is also a founding board member of the United States South African Leader Program and serves on the boards of the Pasadena NAACP and the Institute of Race Relations in South Africa.

He has led State Department missions to Africa, evaluated the Peace Corps in Uganda and Botswana, served on numerous Council on Foreign Relations study groups, and was president of the Los Angeles International Visitor's Council.

Dr. Munger is the author of eleven books, including one novella, on Africa. His books have been published by Oxford University Press, University of Chicago Press, Columbia University Press, and Tafelberg, among others. In addition, he published seventy-five issues of the *Munger Africana Library Notes*, a journal of essays, monographs, and articles on Africa. He has also contributed more than a thousand articles to journals such as *Foreign Affairs, Current History,* and *Geographical Review,* as well as the *Encyclopedia Britannica.*

Questions, comments, and information about chess sets may be sent to:

Ned Munger
Humanities & Social Sciences 228-77
California Institute of Technology
Pasadena, CA 91125